12/12/09

On behalf of the leadership and members of NSCCC, thank you so much for your year of dedication and service through the Music Ministry. We sincerely believe God is glorified and honored by your example of worship and we pray you would continue to strive to live for and please Him as your audience of one...

- North Shore Chinese Christian Church

FOR THE AUDIENCE OF ONE

It's been my honor and privilege to work alongside Mike for many years. I have learned so much about being a worshiper and leading worship from him. His insights and wisdom have profoundly influenced my life. In this book, *For the Audience of One*, Mike has put in print so many of his thoughts and teachings on worship. It's a fantastic book and a must for anyone who is passionate about the worship of God.

TIM HUGHES
AUTHOR, *HERE I AM TO WORSHIP*
WORSHIP LEADER AND SONGWRITER

For the Audience of One is a healthy, focused argument for the centrality and power of worship in the lives of Christians and their churches. I know from personal experience that Mike Pilavachi and the Soul Survivor church really do live out what is written in the book, so it has integrity and practicality built into it.

STEVE NICHOLSON
SENIOR PASTOR, VINEYARD CHRISTIAN CHURCH OF EVANSTON
NATIONAL CHURCH PLANT COORDINATOR
FOR VINEYARD CHURCHES U.S.A.

Mike is the sort of character you'd expect to read about in the Bible alongside all the other heroes of our faith. He's a big man with a big heart, who loves people and adores Jesus. This book will give you a closer glimpse of our Creator.

MARTIN SMITH
ARTIST AND SONGWRITER, DELIRIOUS?

For the Audience of One is a remarkable book that rediscovers worship as the primary purpose of our lives as followers of Christ. In his humorous and unassuming prose, Mike unpacks the importance of worshiping in the midst of the joys, the failures, the successes and the sorrows of life. This book is a great read to be devoured, savored and put into action.

DARLENE ZSCHECH

AUTHOR, *EXTRAVAGANT WORSHIP* AND *KISS OF HEAVEN*
SONGWRITER AND WORSHIP LEADER

FOR THE AUDIENCE OF ONE

MIKE PILAVACHI with CRAIG BORLASE

Regal

From Gospel Light
Ventura, California, U.S.A.

Regal

Published by Regal Books
From Gospel Light
Ventura, California, U.S.A.
Printed in the U.S.A.

Regal Books is a ministry of Gospel Light, a Christian publisher dedicated to serving the local church. We believe God's vision for Gospel Light is to provide church leaders with biblical, user-friendly materials that will help them evangelize, disciple and minister to children, youth and families.

It is our prayer that this Regal book will help you discover biblical truth for your own life and help you meet the needs of others. May God richly bless you.

For a free catalog of resources from Regal Books/Gospel Light, please call your Christian supplier or contact us at 1-800-4-GOSPEL or www.regalbooks.com.

Rights for publishing this book in other languages are contracted by Gospel Light Worldwide, the international nonprofit ministry of Gospel Light. Gospel Light Worldwide also provides publishing and technical assistance to international publishers dedicated to producing Sunday School and Vacation Bible School curricula and books in the languages of the world. For additional information, visit www.gospellightworldwide.org; write to Gospel Light Worldwide, P.O. Box 3875, Ventura, CA 93006; or send an e-mail to info@gospellightworldwide.org.

Revised and updated edition published in 2005 by Regal.
Orginal edition published in 1999 by Hodder and Stoughton Ltd., A Division of Hodder Headline PLC, 338 Euston Road London NW1 3BH.

Cover design by David Griffing
Interior design by Stephen Hahn
Edited by Alex Field

Library of Congress Cataloging-in-Publication Data
Pilavachi, Mike.
   For the audience of one / Mike Pilavachi, with Craig Borlase.
      p. cm.
   ISBN 0-8307-3704-9 (hardcover)
   1. Worship. I. Borlase, Craig. II. Title.

BV10.3.P55 2005
248.3—dc22   2004030613

1   2   3   4   5   6   7   8   9   10   /   11   10   09   08   07   06   05

DEDICATION

To Matt and Beth Redman,
Worship and Evangelism—
a great partnership.

CONTENTS

ACKNOWLEDGMENTS

We would like to thank a number of our friends who have helped us in the writing of this book: David Moloney at Hodder and Stoughton, for his encouragement and patience as each new deadline came and went; Emma Mitchell, for efficiently typing up the transcripts; Rev. Dr. Mark Stibbe, for rescuing us from many theological disasters; Matt Redman, for his many wise and helpful comments. We also recruited a small army to read through the manuscript for any mistakes, and we hope they did a thorough job! They include David Seddon, Ellie Harding, Neil Pearce, Verity Furneaux, Tim Hughes, Martyn Layzell, Liz and Sarah Redman, Dennis and Miriam Layzell, and Carole Japhtha. Also, we must thank Taryn Bibby, who has contributed beyond the call of duty, and Jon Stevens, whose servant heart and commitment to the cause have been inspiring. Thanks to Bishop David Pytches and Mary Pytches for starting us off on our little adventure, and to all the team at Soul Survivor for being you and staying here!

I would also like to thank Bill Greig III and his wonderful family for their friendship and constant encouragement. The Gospel Light and Regal family is an undeserved gift of God to me. Thank you.

FOREWORD

A dynamic occurs when people worship God that you won't find anywhere else on the face of the earth. Worship is about God, worship is for God, and worship is to God. But for some wonderful reason, when we try to give something back to God, so often we end up receiving from Him.

Indeed, worshiping God can usher in all sorts of benefits—an uplifting sense of God's presence, emotional healing, signs and wonders, and even salvation. It's because of these wonderful blessings that we need to keep reminding ourselves constantly that worship is all about Jesus. It's not about what we can get out of it; we don't invest in worship in order to yield a good return. Worship is for God's pleasure and glory. The title of this book says it all—*For the Audience of One.*

At Soul Survivor we've been on a journey of discovery with the whole worship thing. It's always been the main thing as far as we're concerned. Everything else we do flows from that place of relationship with God. While worship obviously concerns the whole of our lives, when we come together, music can be a particularly beautiful expression of it. We started discovering this in a number of ways. Mike, for example, spent his early Christian years heavily impressed by the worship songs of The Fisherfolk. Now that I've heard Mike's worn-out tapes 20 years down the road, it's sometimes a little difficult to comprehend his obsession fully! But the point is that The Fisherfolk was one of the groups that ushered in the rediscovery of the dynamic that occurs when we pour out our love to God through music.

More than anywhere else, we've learned our worship values from the Vineyard Church. I first encountered this brand of intimate, passionate worship at the age of seven, two months after my dad died, and it had a huge impact on me. Since then I have grown up with the wonderful reality that the fearsome, almighty God would beckon even me with His hand of friendship. When we look at this through the window of the Cross, we see that this is the mystery of the universe.

It was in 1989 that we started, with a small group of people, to give over an occasional evening just to worship God and pursue this mystery. We only had the bare essentials—a nearly in-tune acoustic guitar and our voices. If you'd have heard Mike's voice and my guitar playing, you probably wouldn't have stuck around for long, but fortunately for us we knew it wasn't about that! Time after time, when we sought to bring our songs of adoration to God, we'd find ourselves caught up in His amazing presence.

Since those days, we've read loads of books on worship, heard loads of talks and had loads of practice, but in the end I know that if we don't still have the same heart for worship we had back then, we won't make any progress. There was a raw, simple passion to bring our love songs to God and draw near to Him. They were special times, and I sometimes match my heart against them now and wonder if for all my supposed experience, I still have the same heart.

This book looks at many ways we all can learn more about worship and, indeed, become better worshipers, but in the end it reminds us that there's no substitute for having a heart of worship. What exactly is that? For me, it's summed up nowhere better than in Ephesians 5:10: "Find out what pleases the Lord." That's the heart of worship—to want to discover the actions, attitudes and thoughts that are going to make God's heart glad. I hope that this is what has spurred us on to try and discover more about worship—the desire to delight the heart of God with our offerings.

It's definitely an exciting time to be alive. We've had the privilege of being involved in Soul Survivor and of traveling around the world and seeing what God is doing. Everywhere we've been we've witnessed the same thing—a passionate Church, ready to worship God with everything within them. It's far deeper than any music could ever go—these worshipers are serious about taking up the challenge of living the whole of their lives for Jesus.

In a sense, this book is the story of where Soul Survivor's at, in terms of worship. Some of it has been shaped at various meetings and conferences. Much of it has been learned both the hard and the easy ways at Soul Survivor Watford, the church Mike pastors. Loads of this book the old Greek, Mike, formulated inside his own head, with the essential aid of his Bible.

This book does a great job of coming at worship from all sorts of angles. When Mike speaks on worship, he has a real gift for making the subject accessible and entertaining yet deeply challenging. With the help of Craig, Mike's eloquent cowriter, this gift translates brilliantly into writing. I've hung around Mike for a long time now and learned loads about worship from him. Read this book and you'll find out effort-free everything that has taken me 10 years to get out of him!

But in the end, this is not just a book about worship. It is a manual that I pray will help you discover more of what pleases the heart of God, and lead us right to the very heart of worship. Enjoy.

Matt Redman

PREFACE

This whole book is about worship. It is written because my friends at Soul Survivor and I believe that the adoration of God should be the highest calling and top priority for every Christian. In these pages, I've tried to write down some of the things we have learned about worship (often through painful experience).

This book was written because I believe the Bible says that worship is the reason for our existence. This book was also written because, as I have encountered Jesus in worship, He has changed and healed me through it. I remember when John Wimber put on his first conference at Westminster Central Hall in 1983. I had just arrived at St. Andrew's, Chorleywood, the church that would be my home for the next 17 years. Previously, I'd been a deacon in a Baptist church in Harrow and everything that could have gone wrong did go wrong. From relationships to work, it seemed like my life was a disaster. I left the church completely broken, thinking that I was never going to be happy.

As I joined St. Andrew's I heard about the conference that John Wimber was hosting. I went along and was blown away by it. He was funny and his teaching was brilliant. I had never heard anything like it before and the ministry times were amazing too. There were many new things to experience, but what stood out most was the worship; it totally unhinged me. I spent a big part of the week just crying and snuffling my way through songs like "Isn't He Beautiful?" and "Hold Me, Lord, In Your Arms." Many of the songs were incredibly simple and yet totally intimate. As I worshiped, I found healing for my soul. Intimacy set me free. Finally, I had found a way of expressing a relationship with God in which I could feed on the truths that I desperately needed to hear. God loved me. He forgave me. He liked me. As I drank it all in I began to want more, as if it had awoken a thirst deep within.

Since then, I have gradually been finding healing in that place. I have also found power in worship for intercession as well as healing. Also, one of the biggest surprises and joys has been the discovery that worship is also an incredibly effective evangelistic tool. Over the last few years, we have seen thousands of young people come to faith in Jesus as they have found themselves in the midst of a group of passionate worshipers.

But most of all I worship because God deserves it. It is the language of our relationship with Him. Worship is our highest priority.

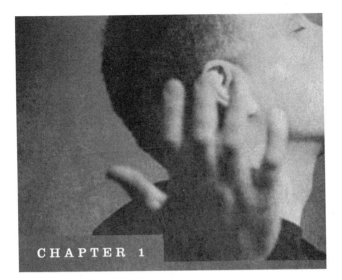

CHAPTER 1

THE HIGHEST PRIORITY

However we approach the issue, there is no altering the highest priority of humankind. We can try as hard as we like, but we'll never twist the definition of our purpose on Earth to read, "I am here to shop" or "I exist to make money." Sure, shopping and making a living are part of the fabric of our lives, but they can never be the main reason that we are here. That place is reserved for something special: worship.

Worship is the highest priority of the human race. It is what we were created for and it is why we are here. Worship is our defining characteristic. The big question throughout our history has never been, Will we worship? Instead, the issue we've always focused on, what will we worship? Think about it: We all worship something. Hindus worship, Buddhists worship, Muslims worship, materialists worship, Marxists worship and even Yankee fans worship something or someone. This has been true for centuries, and it provides much common ground between ourselves and that cast of thousands we read so much about in the Bible, the Israelites. Throughout their history, as depicted in the Old Testament, if they didn't worship the Lord their God, they very soon found other things to worship.

But the priority of worship doesn't stop there. Not only has God made it our highest priority, but He has also called us to a lifestyle of worship, to be at it around the clock. Does that mean that we are never without our iPod, blasting inspirational praise and worship tunes? Thankfully not, as God has a bigger idea of what He wants from us. Jesus said in Mark 12:29-31 that the greatest commandment in the whole law is that we love the Lord our God with all our heart, soul, mind and strength. That is a commandment to worship. To love the Lord our God with all that we have is to develop and maintain an intimate relationship with our Maker. Above all else, that's what God wants.

My background is in the Anglican Church; I've been working within it for years. There are some aspects of the Anglican liturgy that I love, because they are so rich. The prayer of thanksgiving, which we say when we break the bread, reads, "It is our duty and our joy, at all times and in all places to give [God] thanks and praise, holy Father, heavenly King, almighty and eternal God."[1]

Sometimes thanking God seems a little removed from the more obvious expressions of joy—when did you last hear of drugs that made you feel thankful all over? Sometimes thanking God may feel more like duty than joy, but it is both our duty and our joy. Throughout the centuries, from the Old Testament until today, Bible teachers have stressed this point. While reading up for this book, I came across a quote from Graham Kendrick, suggesting that if we really worshiped as we should, there wouldn't be any need for evangelism.[2] Now, the prospect of an evangelism-free life could have you pounding the wall either with rage or delight. But the point is that if we really worshiped as we should, if we loved God as we will love Him in heaven, our worship would be so inspiring that people would flock to Him.

In his book *Celebration of Discipline*, Richard Foster says, "The divine priority is worship first, service second."[3] When we commit ourselves first and foremost to worshiping God as He deserves, then the acts of service will follow. Put another way, God desires intimacy with us first and foremost. Put yet another way: Do you remember Mary and Martha (see Luke 10:38-42)? Which one did Jesus commend? Jesus commended Mary instead of Martha because she sat and listened to His words, despite the fact that Martha had busied herself with all the work and preparation. In other words, "When God has our hearts, our hands will surely follow!"

A DEFINITION OF WORSHIP

Perhaps this would be a good time to get back to basics and find out exactly what worship is. Put simply, worship is to give God what is rightfully His. And what does the Creator of the universe deserve? How about adoration, praise, thanks and love? Those are a few of the things that He is worth, and they help define the way that we should be relating to Him.

Another defining characteristic of worship is that it must come before everything else. That doesn't mean that we ought to have our ears permanently clamped between two worship-blaring headphones. What it means is that we need to have our hearts right. If we are first of all lovers of God, people

> **If we are first of all lovers of God, people who are devoted to praising and worshiping Him, then our deeds will be powered by the right motives.**

who are devoted to praising and worshiping Him, then our deeds will be powered by the right motives. When we get our priorities right and put the worship of God first, then everything else falls into place. When we put other things first—even other good things; other good, Christian things—then everything falls apart. It's as simple as that. St. Augustine (a very ancient guy) had a great phrase. He said: "Love, and do what you like."[4] By that he meant that when we truly love God, we'll want to do things that please Him.

At Soul Survivor we believe that our first calling is to be worshipers of God. When the people of Israel turned away from God and replaced Him with idols, everything fell apart. We are trying to avoid that particular trap by making God the central focus of our lives.

We were created to worship God; we were made with a yearning for intimacy with our Maker. He made us in His image so that we could have relationship with Him. When, for whatever reason, we turn from God, we will always try to replace Him with something else. Our God substitute could be anything from sex to ambition to other religious figures. Whenever the Israelites took time out from God, they were sure to end up sick, fighting or in trouble. When they went back to God, things always got better. Relationship with God is the heart's true home.

In Jeremiah 2:13 the prophet proclaims the following words: "My people have committed two sins: They have forsaken me, the spring of living water, and have dug their own cisterns, broken cisterns that cannot hold water." If we forsake God, the spring of living water, and try to find our own water, we're digging our own cisterns. This is a helpful picture, as it shows God as a life source, a vital component to our survival. When we ignore Him, we find other things to serve as our life source. The trouble is that you have to go a pretty long way to beat the "spring of living water." Tapping into substandard and impure substitutes guarantees us nothing but trouble. We eventually find that all our God substitutes are like broken cisterns. They don't hold water and cannot quench our thirst.

Often the things out of which we try to squeeze satisfaction are good in their rightful places, but their rightful places are where they need to stay. For example, how on earth could football, shopping or ambition ever act as the main purpose of life? Even if you put them all together and form a syndicate, these things are pale and narrow in comparison to God's great richness and diversity. No, we were made by God and for God. He gave us plenty of toys, but He only gave us one purpose.

MY STORY

Since I've been a Christian, God has healed me of many things, but perhaps the most amazing was my tendency towards possessiveness. This was something I had to get healed of when I first became a

Christian. My background contains a fair amount of brokenness, and because of that I used to get possessive about people, believing that they didn't like me and would leave at any time. It was a fear that drove me, and I can point to things that happened when I was very young to identify its roots.

When I was five and it was time for me to go to school, I had my first shock. I hadn't mixed with any other kids until then, and I did not have any English-speaking friends. I could only speak Greek at the time, and I can still remember my first day at school. I can see myself sitting on my bed and my mum tying up my shoelaces, putting these strange clothes on me and then taking me to school. I remember the tension that had been building up in the house, and how when I arrived at school all the other kids seemed so much bigger than I was. I was frightened by the screaming and shouting on the playground. I was unable to understand what was going on.

For months I was crippled by shyness because I couldn't speak English. I couldn't communicate, and all I did during the breaks was walk up and down the playground on my own. I was scared of all the other students. They would play football; and I would long to join in, but I couldn't, because I simply didn't know how to play. Years later, as I started to build relationships, those feelings of isolation and loneliness resurfaced whenever I began to make new friends. I would do anything to keep them as friends, and I was in what seemed like a perpetual state of panic. If I saw any of my friends getting on well with anyone else, something inside me would knot up and I would panic, convinced that they didn't care about

> **I felt as though other people always understood each other better than I could and that I was destined to feel like an outsider for the rest of my life.**

me and would soon leave me alone. I felt as though other people always understood each other better than I could, that they were much happier without me and that I was destined to feel like an outsider for the rest of my life.

I developed a safety strategy to keep myself from ever getting hurt: If I felt that someone was about to reject me, I would reject him or her first. I would withdraw and punish them with my silence. At one point I went for two years without speaking to anyone in my class at school, and I hardly spoke to anyone in my family. I completely withdrew into myself and was consumed by my inner feelings. My parents didn't know what to do. They tried to get me to talk to my brother and sister, but I just couldn't.

It has taken years of finding Jesus as the source of my life to move on from those feelings. I feel like I am the living embodiment of the phrase "broken cisterns"—I know that on my own I simply would not have made it this far. Finding Jesus meant finding life, although it didn't mean getting fixed immediately. Even now, though I have come so far, I am still vulnerable to some watered-down versions of those old feelings. But when those old feelings resurface, I have a choice to make: Do I turn to God or do I run away? Turning to God means looking to Him to affirm me. It means finding Him as the spring of living water as I pour out my heart in the intimacy of worship.

Notes

1. The Archbishop's Council for the Church of England, "Prayer A," *Common Prayer: Daily Worship, www.cofe.angli can.org,* 2000-2004. http://www.cofe.anglican.org/worship /liturgy/commonworship/texts/hc/prayera.html (accessed December 21, 2004).

2. Graham Kendrick, *Learning to Worship as a Way of Life* (Minneapolis, MN: Bethany House Publishers, 1985) n.p.

3. Richard Foster, *Celebration of Discipline: The Path to Spiritual Growth* (San Francisco: HarperSanFrancisco, 1988) p. 161.

4. Saint Augustine, "Saint Augustine Quotes," *BrainyQuote*. 2004. http://www.brainyquote.com/quotes/authors/s/saint _augustine.html (accessed December 20, 2004).

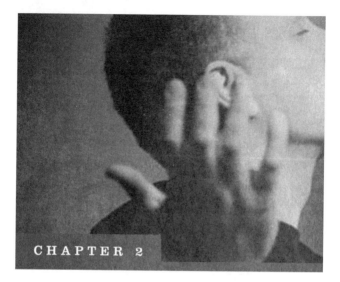

CHAPTER 2

SACRIFICE IN WORSHIP

Sacrifice—it may not be the most exciting of concepts.
In fact, this whole sacrifice thing is in need of a severe
public image overhaul. Right now it's all too drab,
mooching around somewhere between "charitable
giving" and giving your seat to old people on buses.
Drop the s-word into a conversation with most people
today and the chances are you'll receive a blank
stare by way of return. Sacrifice has almost become
an irrelevancy. Maybe with a few nips and tucks, a
glitzy advertising campaign and some clever product
placement we can make it hip. Perhaps not.

You see, sacrifice isn't supposed to be fun. It isn't even supposed to be rewarding; it is most definitely a one-way street. In these days of personal freedom and the right to direct our own lives, one-way streets are most definitely out. So we have a problem on our hands: God likes sacrifice; we don't. Oh dear.

Sacrifice has always been found right at the heart of worship; it is, if you like, one of the spokes of the wheel. It is inextricably linked to that other favorite of ours, obedience. Throughout the Old Testament, we read story after story that detail the many ways in which the Israelites would offer sacrifices to the Lord, obeying His commands to do so. In all but one of the main Hebrew festivals, the sacrifice of lambs, goats, doves, grain or drink was a key part. Those festivals were not a million miles away from the big rock festivals we have today; people got together, had a good time and gave away something that they valued—animals, in the case of the Hebrew festivals.

The Hebrew festivals weren't all miserable affairs—they existed to continue communication between the Creator and the created. On some occasions, the focus was the celebration of God's goodness, while on others it would center on the process of mourning or the act of asking God to intervene in a specific situation. But all those festivals had sacrifice and obedience in common.

SACRIFICE

I love the passage in 2 Chronicles 7. Solomon and the people of Israel had spent years building the Temple in Jerusalem, which was going to be the permanent home for their previously mobile altar.

Such an important artifact needed a pretty special home—hence the prolonged building campaign—designed by a pretty special architect. It was God Himself who provided Solomon with the plans, detailing everything from the foundations to the furnishings. As Solomon and his builders followed God's specifications, God sent a message to them (and to us today) that worship is always on His terms, not on ours. If God felt ambivalent toward that whole Temple concept, then He wouldn't have gotten involved. As it was, He was specific and detailed in His instructions. It's the same with our worship: God likes it and He wants to make sure that we get it right.

That idea seems to conflict with contemporary thought. Today, we subscribe to the belief that worship is a personal choice. If I want to worship God by banging a drum, then surely I am free to do so. Likewise, I cannot criticize those who opt for High Church liturgy and structured worship. This is only part of the truth however. Yes, it is wrong for us to try to make others worship on our terms, but that also extends to God; we don't have the last word in the direction of our own worship of God. What we have to do is worship our Maker on His own terms. After all, if the worship is for Him, then surely we

> **What we have to do is worship our Maker on His own terms. After all, if the worship is for Him, then surely we should pause to inquire about His preferences and His tastes, and be a little less consumed with ours.**

should pause to inquire about His preferences and His tastes, and be a little less consumed with ours. Lord, how would you like us to worship You today? should be the constant question of our hearts.

Before that sets you off in a panic, consider God's infinite size and creativity, as well as the fact that you have been made in His image. Chances are, the terms He gives you for how you are to worship Him will not be totally alien to you. Anyway, the Lord does not seem to be too bothered about whether it is with an organ or a drum, but He is very concerned about whether it is from the heart.

Back to the story: Once the Temple was finished and the Israelites had brought the Ark of the Covenant to it, they dedicated it. Chapter 7 starts just after Solomon had prayed an amazing prayer of dedication:

> When Solomon finished praying, fire came down from heaven and consumed the burnt offering and the sacrifices, and the glory of the Lord filled the temple. The priests could not enter the temple of the Lord because the glory of the Lord filled it. When all the Israelites saw the fire coming down and the glory of the Lord above the temple, they knelt on the pavement with their faces to the ground, and they worshiped and gave thanks to the Lord saying, "He is good; his love endures forever." Then the king and all the people offered sacrifices before the Lord.

And King Solomon offered a sacrifice of twenty-two thousand head of cattle and a hundred and twenty thousand sheep and goats. So the king and all the people dedicated the temple of God. The priests took their positions, as did the Levites with the Lord's musical instruments, which King David had made for praising the Lord and which were used when he gave thanks, saying, "His love endures forever." Opposite the Levites, the priests blew their trumpets, and all the Israelites were standing (2 Chron. 7:1-6).

This was some worship session. It tells us so much that too quick a reading of this passage could cause us to miss some of the juiciest bits. The whole Temple project had been carried out on a grand scale. The labor force topped 153,600 men; there was enough gold inside the Temple to sink the *Titanic*; and the dedication service didn't disappoint either. The king offered a sacrifice magnificent enough to feed tens of thousands of people for two weeks (see 1 Kings 8:65).

Can you imagine that? It wasn't a potluck barbecue thrown to say thank-you to the workers. It was a massive fellowship offering. The size of the sacrifice was magnificent. David once mused regarding an animal sacrifice he had made, "Shall I offer to God that which cost me nothing?" The answer of course is obvious. Worship is meant to cost something.

That leaves us in a bit of a quandary: How well would you be received if you were to enter your local church leading an exodus of livestock from the local farms? Of course, we know that Jesus' death on the cross was the once-for-all, perfect sacrifice for our salvation, but still, that leaves us on the giving end of something far less tangible: the sacrifice of our own lives.

Back to Solomon as the glory of the Lord descended. People knelt on the ground with their faces to the dirt, and the priests could not perform their duties. They couldn't enter the Temple either, as it was so filled with God's presence, His Godness. The timing of this arrival was no coincidence, and it is yet another piece of evidence that points towards the conclusion that the glory of God comes in the place of sacrifice.

That is not the only example of the link between God's glory and our sacrifice. At one point, King David left the Ark of the Lord at the home of a guy called Obed-Edom, the Gittite, instead of taking it back to Jerusalem (see 2 Sam. 6:9-10). The Ark remained there for three months, and the Lord blessed Obed-Edom and his entire household.

Isn't that interesting? The Ark of the Lord's presence at Obed-Edom's place was enough for the Lord to bless him.

> Now King David was told, "The Lord has blessed the household of Obed-Edom and everything he has, because of the ark of God." So David went down and brought up the ark of God from the house of Obed-Edom to the City of David with rejoicing. When those who were carrying the ark of the Lord had taken six steps, he sacrificed a bull and a fattened calf. David, wearing a linen ephod, danced before the Lord with all his might, while he and the entire house of Israel brought up the ark of the Lord with shouts and the sound of trumpets (2 Sam. 6:12-15).

Michal, the daughter of Saul, watched David from the window, despising him in her heart. It's interesting that David danced before the Lord with all of his might after they brought the Ark of the Covenant from Obed-Edom's house to Jerusalem. Now we don't know how far away Obed-Edom lived from Jerusalem, but even if it had been only a few miles, the journey would have been something of an epic. You see, it wasn't just a case of hitching up the old Ark and trotting off down the road. The text indicates that, "When those who were carrying the ark of the Lord had taken six steps, he [David] sacrificed a bull and a fattened calf" (v. 13). It is quite possible that they performed this sacrifice every six steps.

At the beginning it would probably have been great, a regular parade. After a while, though, the novelty was bound to have worn off. Not only would the length of time it took have been frustrating, but also there was the issue of economics: Those cattle had to come from somewhere. They came at a price. Once the journey was over, David made the final sacrifice, stripping down to his linen ephod and dancing before his God. True, unrestrained joy in God is birthed in the place of sacrificial worship.

You can view the history of the Old Testament sacrifices as preparation for the life and (sacrificial) death of Jesus. Once He went to the cross and the obligation to offer sacrifices of bulls and goats and lambs in order to cover sin was through; Jesus died to wash us clean from our sins once and for all. In a sense, that sacrificial system died when Jesus died; He was the ultimate sacrifice and none could better Him. At the same time, in another sense, the sacrificial system didn't end there, because we're commanded in the New Testament to offer sacrifices of praise (see Heb. 13:15-16). Also, in Romans 12:1, Paul says, "Therefore, I urge you, brothers, in view of God's mercy, to offer your bodies as living sacrifices, holy and pleasing to God—this is your spiritual act of worship." That's it: It's not lambs, doves or cows anymore. It's my body. It's your body. It's our bodies, acting as living sacrifices. That is our spiritual act of worship. This time, however, we do it not to earn God's favor, in an attempt to win His love or salvation, but to express our love and adoration, as a response to His salvation.

When I remind myself of this, it stirs me up again. I want to give Him the lot and hold nothing of myself back. If we have this understanding when taking part in worship and when leading it, then our songs will take their proper place. God's glory often comes when we sacrifice. I want to get closer to God and be able to give more of myself as a sacrifice so that I can see His glory.

OBEDIENCE

Looking through the Bible lately, I've been struck by how worship is presented through lifestyle. Read between the lines, and certain stories reveal a subtext that promotes what I can only describe as radical obedience. Radical obedience isn't about the way you sing songs; being radical is about the life you live. That makes for some serious potential obedience.

I suppose the first hint towards radical obedience came in the Sermon on the Mount, in which Jesus delivered His manifesto for good living. When He suggested turning the other cheek, going the extra mile and donating the second shirt, He was laying down the law for a new way of life. His metaphors all screamed out the instruction to be truly radical, to live a different way.

Jesus didn't say, "If you love me, you will sing the latest songs." What He said was, "If you love me, you will obey what I command" (John 14:15). There's so much for us to learn from this, and it starts with that prickly little word: "obedience."

Obedience is a biblical principle. As we become slaves to Jesus Christ, we find freedom. It's as servants of God that we find our true selves, and it's in pouring our lives out that we can worship. Radical obedience is squaring up to Jesus' words, "If you love me, you will obey what I command."

> **It's as servants of God that we find our true selves, and it's in pouring our lives out that we can worship.**

Being radical isn't about worshiping with the drums, a guitar and a bass; neither is it about dancing around waving banners or worshiping face down. It's about obedience. How can we get it right during the Sunday service if we can't sort it out during the week? How can there ever be radical worship in church, if day by day, out there, I'm not acting in obedience? If I'm not seeking to deny myself, take up my cross and follow Him? We must learn to leave behind our own interests and agendas, and choose to serve others first. Then we will be His disciples. If believing

Jesus' statement in John 14:15 does not affect how we act at work, home or school, then unfortunately they're just words.

The danger here is that at this point you might promptly put this book down to collect dust. "Oh Mike," you might say, "stick to those funny little stories you tell." The trouble is that this issue won't go away. If we don't learn to obey God's commands, then we will struggle. It doesn't all have to be doom and gloom though, for as Jesus pointed out, "Whoever finds his life will lose it, and whoever loses his life for my sake will find it" (Matthew 10:39). Believe me, when Jesus talks about finding life, He means it, in all the technicolor glory that was first intended.

Joyful sacrifice is a theme that runs deep throughout the whole Bible, surfacing with particular momentum in Luke 19: "Jesus entered Jericho and was passing through. A man was there by the name of Zacchaeus; he was a chief tax collector and was wealthy" (vv. 1-2).

What does that mean? It certainly does not mean that he worked for the government, that he was a respectable, upright civil servant. He worked for the occupying power, the enemy. He was regarded as a traitor, and not just a low-grade one at that. No, Zacchaeus was high up in the traitor business, rising through the ranks to reach the position of chief tax collector. As such, his job description was fairly simple: take money from his own people, give some to the Romans, take a few bribes and pocket whatever he fancied. His social circle would have consisted of other social outcasts. He was certainly wealthy, probably lonely and quite possibly unhappy.

"He [Zacchaeus] wanted to see who Jesus was, but being a short man he could not, because of the crowd. So he ran ahead and climbed a sycamore-fig tree to see him, since Jesus was coming that way" (vv. 3-4). Zacchaeus had heard about Jesus and wanted to see who He was. So, he climbed up a sycamore tree, which was a pretty strange thing for a tax collector to do; but he was desperate, and the tree was his only chance.

"When Jesus reached the spot, he looked up and said to him, 'Zacchaeus, come down immediately'" (v. 5). Now I don't know exactly what happened there, but I just wonder whether when Jesus said that to him, Zacchaeus thought, *Oh no, He's going to call me out; He's seen me and He knows who I am.* And the crowd around, who would have known him, might have been saying, "Go on, if you're the Messiah, slay him."

But then Jesus would have stunned them all when He said, "I must stay at your house today" (v. 5). It's brilliant. Only Jesus would say something like that. All around him there were the religious leaders, the Pharisees and other respectable people, and Jesus looked up a tree and basically said, "I've seen you, Zacchaeus, and I know your name. I know your name, so come down; I'm inviting myself over for dinner." In the Scriptures, eating together was seen as an intimate act (which is why, in Song of Songs 2:4, it says, "He has taken me to the banquet hall, and his banner over me is love"). Jesus wasn't announcing His intention to check out Zacchaeus's best hors d'oeuvres and fashionable interior decor; He was telling him that He wanted to share fellowship with him.

> All the people saw this and began to mutter, "He has gone to be the guest of a 'sinner.'" But Zacchaeus stood up and said to the Lord, "Look, Lord! Here and now I give half of my possessions to the poor, and if I have cheated anybody out of anything, I will pay back four times the amount." Jesus said to

him, "Today salvation has come to this house, because this man, too, is a son of Abraham. For the Son of Man came to seek and to save what was lost" (Luke 19:7-10).

The fruit of what Jesus said was that Zacchaeus welcomed Him gladly and took Him home. If we really know what we've been saved from, as Zacchaeus did, then we welcome Jesus in. And because Jesus' simple act of asking to go to his house was in such stark contrast to the usual treatment that he received from others, Zacchaeus responded with amazing, generous and overflowing obedience. Giving away half of his possessions and repaying four times the amount he had swindled from others was no small feat. Neither was Jesus' response: "Today, salvation has come to this house." Salvation didn't come when Zacchaeus declared his intention to relieve himself of so much of his wealth; it actually came much earlier when Jesus told him to get down from the tree and put the kettle on. It is not our sacrifice that saves us; rather, that sacrifice should be an automatic, joyful response to being forgiven. Zacchaeus's generosity was the fruit of his salvation. Our sacrifice of obedience isn't out of duty;

it's out of a massive overflow of our love for Jesus. God is calling us to be radical Christians. We too have received His salvation; now it's time to respond.

God calls us to this response, not that He may squeeze more out of us, but that He may put more into us. This is the secret of a joy-filled life: We are no longer our own; we are His. Jesus' own life was a perfect model of obedience. He obeyed His Father, and He told us that if we love Him, we will obey His commands. It's as simple as that.

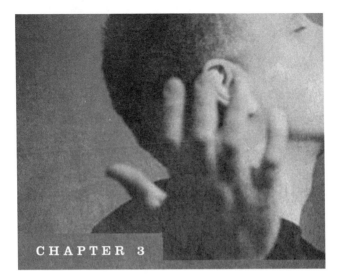

THE LANGUAGE
OF WORSHIP

We worship in many different ways—through creativity and dedication, expression and commitment, songs and work. It's like a love affair. If I asked you how you knew you were loved, chances are that you would come up with evidence ranging from gifts and words to sacrifices and actions. There is also another way that we know that we are loved: by how we feel. This state is hard to describe as it belongs to the strange realm of the heart. Traditional, logical explanations fail to work in this arena. For example, how ridiculous does it sound to describe a kiss as the mutual oral exchange of molecules and saliva? Description here is difficult.

In the same way that there are different kinds of love, there are different kinds of worship: the worship that comes from our lips, the worship that comes from our lives and the worship that comes from our hearts. Within each area there are codes and formats, methods of expression and limitations of use. Together they make up the language of worship.

THE LANGUAGE OF OUR HEARTS

A. W. Tozer said, "True worship is to be so personally and hopelessly in love with God, that the idea of a transfer of affection never even remotely exists."[1]

Over the years I have seen people change radically because they have met Jesus, fallen in love with Him and expressed that in passionate, intimate worship and in radical repentance. Some years ago at a Soul Survivor festival in England, we were in the middle of a time of musical worship, when a young man came up and handed a knife to me and said, "Please take this. I don't want it anymore; I want to follow Jesus." A few minutes later another young man came up and handed me a set of brass knuckles and said the same thing. Not long after that a third young man gave me some condoms and asked me to dispose of them, as he now wanted to live for Jesus. For a while I was puzzled. I hadn't even preached yet! I had not taught that if you want to follow Jesus, you should not stab people, leave marks on their faces or have sex outside of marriage.

What happened? During the worship, they met with God—I saw the results myself—it truly affected them. Once they had touched the eternal, they no longer had the desire to waste their affections on the little things. Worship can be like that; it can be the language of the heart—an unheard, untranslatable tongue that communicates directly and profoundly.

I have worked with youth for so long that I have probably reached my "sell by" date. One of the hardest things I have to do as a youth worker is to give the sex talk. It isn't that the subject is embarrassing to talk about. It is more that it comes up with such monotonous regularity. I could give the sex talk in my sleep. The point is that I wonder if it makes a lot of difference. I have noticed, however, that when people really meet Jesus and have that intimate exchange with Him in worship, they want to do what pleases Him. There has been a transfer of affections. The word that the Bible uses to describe this is "repentance." "Repentance" literally means "the action or process of repenting or turning from sin."[2] Repentance is also worship; it is responding to Jesus by choosing to live a life of obedience to Him.

Tozer also went on to examine the issue of idolatry: the ideas that we are created to worship and that we will worship either God or other gods. "The essence of idolatry," Tozer also said, "is the entertainment of thoughts about God that are unworthy of him."[3] Now this one had me confused. *What has thinking got to do with idolatry?* I thought. The lights came on when I realized that thinking an unworthy thought about God makes that thought an idol; it downgrades God's worth and means that we construct something that is not truly God. Our task is not simply to turn from false idols but also to banish misconceptions about who God is.

THE LANGUAGE OF OUR HANDS

Question: Is it possible to express passionate, intimate devotion and adoration without the use of our bodies? **Answer:** Yes, but you have to be in a coma.

Many of the words used in Hebrew to describe acts of worship are very interesting; nearly all of them signify a specific physical posture. In the Psalms, so many of the commands are to do physical things. We are all familiar with phrases like "I lift my eyes up to the mountains," "lift up your heads to the coming King" and "I lift up my hands." These are physical expressions of praise and thanksgiving. Alongside these are those expressions that express our humility and God's sovereignty, the kneeling down in verses such as, "Come, let us bow down in worship, let us kneel before the Lord our Maker" (Psalm 95:6). On a slightly more intense level, we find the physical expressions of tearing clothes and wearing sackcloth and ashes when in mourning (see Matt. 11:21).

It seems pretty clear from the Bible that the Israelites were a very physical group of people when it came to worshiping God. We know from their worship that they weren't shy about using their bodies (remember that whole loincloth thing that David had going as he danced in front of the sacrifice?). Still, drawing on cultural reference points from the past can often be a red herring when it comes to the present. Relevance seems to fade severely over the years, and of course, no church would want to make people do things they were uncomfortable with. I can explain this better by giving you an example. I struggle with the whole dancing issue. Not having been blessed with a thoroughly accurate sense of rhythm, I tend to look rather like a drunken Elvis impersonator, on the rare occasions that I get up and strut my stuff. At times my inner monologue contains a battle between the belief that dance was a pivotal act in Old Testament worship and the knowledge that my moves would have people doubled over in hysterics, as my dancing conjured thoughts about both Elvis and muscular spasms in the same descriptive sentence.

Obviously it's stupid to use worship as an excuse for putting on a show to impress the locals. However, there is a case for the argument that spending a worship time sitting down with arms folded and a glum look on our faces is perhaps not the best indication of a heart that is on fire for God. We know from studies in communication and sociology that we actually express far more through our actions and the movement of our bodies than our words.

In the Hebrew culture there was a great understanding of who we are as human beings. Instead of subscribing to the belief that we are spirits trapped inside our bodies, there was a common belief that spirit and flesh are mirror images of each other. The inference of this is that our bodies are meant to

> **Sometimes we say that dancing or raising our hands in worship is not part of our culture. These are man-made barriers. We were all made to laugh, dance, sing and do all manner of things to express joy.**

reflect what is in our hearts, especially when we are worshiping our Maker. Fake, outward manifestations, such as a plastered-on smile, can be used to try and convince others, but that is nothing more than hypocrisy. At the same time, if the love of God is in our hearts, we're meant to (in fact, we're almost commanded to) express that through our bodies. Sometimes we say that, for example, dancing or raising our hands in worship is not part of our culture, that we're not "that kind of Christian." But these are man-made barriers. We were all made to laugh, dance, sing and do all manner of things to express joy. In explaining this, we come across a central point to understanding the language of worship: This language is not simply saying the words, "I bless You, Lord. I give You thanks." It is a matter of using the whole body to express those things as well. Many times in Scripture we see that hands and hearts are mentioned in the same breath, particularly in the context of worship. Psalm 24:3-4 is just one example: "Who may stand in his holy place? He who has clean hands and a pure heart." It was assumed that if God touched your heart, you would express this through your body and also through acts of obedience.

Such a style of expression has of late been finding its way back into the Church. But we have only just begun to do this, and there is a long way to go before we can declare that we have fully captured the spirit of David as he danced before his God. His wife may have been offended at his behavior, but her problems should not become our defense. She was Saul's daughter, and the dancing incident was one of many things that caused her to look down on David. Bitterly she said to him, "How the king of Israel has distinguished himself today, disrobing in the sight of the slave girls of his servants as any vulgar fellow would" (2 Sam, 6:20). David's reply was essentially "You ain't seen nothing yet," as he ranted on about becoming even more undignified. He was worshiping in his underpants, and he threatened to go further. He was willing to do whatever it took for him to be able to express his devotion to God. He allowed himself to be totally abandoned in his praise and thanksgiving. Sometimes that's a decision we all have to make: to do whatever is necessary to express our feelings for God.

I remember when Martin Smith from Delirious? told me how bad he was at dancing. Quite why he chose to tell me, I'm not sure—he must have felt safe, having viewed my Elvis impersonations. But if we're really honest, he still is pretty terrible. Well, he decided at one stage that he was fed up with not dancing and that he was going to go for it. He began in his church, having felt that he didn't want to be hindered any longer. So he started, choosing to run around the church hall. He ran around for a bit and then thought, *I don't care what anyone thinks,* so he started to jump.

Now maybe you've seen him jumping when he's on stage. For Martin, overcoming his psychological barriers in order to worship further was a conscious decision. In our churches we need to encourage others to do this, without nagging them. That doesn't mean we condemn as sinners those who don't do the same as we do, but it does mean explaining that sometimes worship is an act of the will. Sometimes it means making the decision to worship with my body, as well as with my mind and my lips.

THE LANGUAGE OF INTIMACY

The heart of worship is intimacy. All worship roads should lead to intimacy, and it is in the place of intimacy that we receive power to live a life of sacrificial, devoted worship in the world. There's a chance that all of this could seem slightly irrelevant to some people. To many, the act of intimately adoring our Father comes second to doing things for him. While I do not wish to deny the importance of practical deeds, I'm reminded of the story in John 12 of Jesus' meeting with the sinful woman Mary Magdalene. She poured a jar of very expensive perfume (it was reported to have been worth a year's wages) over Jesus' feet. Her abandonment riled Judas to the point that he complained that the perfume could have been put to better use. There were plenty of other worthy causes that could have used the cash. And today, there are always evangelistic missions to be funded, churches to be extended and projects to realize. At the same time, there is also Jesus. He looks for the same response from us that He found in Mary: waste. He wants us to waste everything we have on Him: our money, our talents, our time and our energy. The place of offering is there at His feet, and it is always open to our approach.

Notes

1. A. W. Tozer, *Tozer on Worship and Entertainment: Selected Excerpts,* comp. James L. Snyder (Camp Hill, PA: Christian Publications, 1997), n.p.

2. *Merriam-Webster's Dictionary Collegiate Dictionary*, 11th ed., s.v. "repentance."

3. A. W. Tozer, *The Knowledge of the Holy–Reissue* (San Francisco, CA: HarperSanFrancisco, 1978), p. 3.

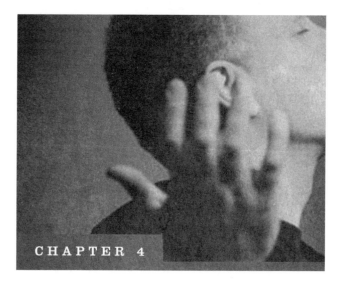

CHAPTER 4

THE FRUIT OF WORSHIP: PART 1—HEALING

We worship because He deserves it, because worship is the expression of intimacy with Him. Whenever we worship Him, there is a consequence; at times that means we find healing, but it can also mean that our levels of holiness increase. We will look at both of these fruits in the next two chapters.

The title I've chosen for this book hints at the idea that worship is not supposed to be for us, but for Him. It is not a question of our gaining anything from worshiping Him, because it hardly matters if we find a particular session exciting or fun. Worship is God's, not ours. However, despite the ridiculous nature of a comment like "I really got a lot out of the worship today," there seems to be some kind of loophole. You see, when we worship, we always get something back. God cannot be outdone in terms of generosity. As we give, we always get something back, particularly in worship. However, it's not worship if we decide that we will worship in order to get something back: That's an exchange. God's into giving, not exchanging.

CHANGE

When I became a Christian, I believed that change would come rapidly. Part of this stemmed from the fact that my Greek heritage had endowed me with the ability to grow in just under an afternoon what for most teenage boys would amount to a week's worth of facial hair. The fruits of the Spirit, I logically concluded, were bound to be like my beard: quick to arrive and reasonably easy to maintain. I needed a fair amount of sorting out when I first met God, and I had it in mind to get it all done by Christmas, leaving me ready to take on the conversion of England by Easter. Of course, it didn't happen.

You know what they say about watched kettles? It's the same deal with change: It seems as if it takes an eternity when you watch for it like a hawk. Change usually takes time, and I've discovered that it is a very gradual process, not something that happens overnight. I've also noticed that when I look at myself intently, picking over every move, mood and reaction, I usually see no sign of change at all. When I reach the end of a week and wonder how much more loving, tender, compassionate and generally brilliant I am, the answer is usually zero. But things do start to happen when I forget about myself and look at God. Somehow the Holy Spirit sneaks up and changes me. Something will have happened despite the fact that it seems to take a very long time and even though there is an awful long way to go.

HEALING AND WHOLENESS

Doctors are labeling many of the problems that we experience today—our sicknesses and illnesses—as being psychosomatic. The physical symptoms can have psychological roots, and (based on the belief that as many as 60 percent of illnesses are stress related) many surgeries are now employing professional counselors to help patients deal with stress. When the Bible talks about a root of bitterness, we talk about a bad self-image. This could be a contributing factor in any number of conditions, from asthma to arthritis, cancer to colitis.

It is interesting that lately, as a Church, we in the United Kingdom have seen far more emotional healing than we have seen physical. Some people have viewed this as a reason for sadness, explaining that living in "miracle days," when the dead rise and the blind see on a daily basis, is a sure sign that revival is close at hand. We do long to see more physical healing, signs and miracles. However, let us give thanks for what God is doing in binding up the brokenhearted. Often God is healing the cause rather than the symptom.

God is a God who heals. Over the last few years, many Christians have rediscovered the practice of healing ministry, realizing that it is permissible to ask (and expect) God to heal. When Jesus walked the earth 2,000 years ago, He told the disciples that they would do the same things as He (and even greater) when He had gone to heaven. In the book of Acts, we see the disciples casting out demons, healing people from various diseases and setting people free in the name of Jesus. We see that praying for healing is one of the main indications that we are following Jesus. God can heal people when we lay hands on people and pray for them, but He also heals us when we worship. It may take a long time, but when we adore Him, we are set free.

My friend and colleague Matt Redman was part of the youth group that I inherited when I started to work at St. Andrew's, Chorleywood. He was 13; and soon after I came on board, he told me that when he was 7, his father had committed suicide. His father sent Matt and his brother and sisters a note that said they would be better off without him. Then, two years later, his mother remarried, and after a period when things were good, everything eventually went horribly wrong. Matt blamed himself for his father's death and was afraid that if he said how unhappy he was, he would be the cause of another family breakup.

Eventually the pressure got so great that Matt told me how bad he was feeling. In the years that followed, I saw Matt's pain, his struggles and insecurities. I saw God heal Matt in an incredible way. It took many years, and it was as he worshiped that God healed him. If Matt has an anointing for worship leading now, I'm sure it's because he genuinely found God's healing in worship.

Many of the songs that he writes now come from that same place, and that is why they speak to people. One of his songs starts like this:

> I will offer up my life in spirit and truth,
> pouring out the oil of love as my worship to
>   You.
> In surrender I must give my every part
> Lord, receive the sacrifice of a broken heart.[1]

A broken heart was not written there to rhyme with "every part": It was written because that's exactly where Matt was coming from. We all need to learn to give our sacrifice when we are in pain.

To worship is to find healing. Some of us have had to live with all sorts of things that have thrown us off course. As we devote ourselves to worship, we get drawn up like a plant toward the sun, the heat and the light of God's love healing us, leaving us upright instead of bent over in pain.

A NEW PERSPECTIVE

To worship is also to gain a new perspective on life. Sometimes we can almost cherish our negative attitudes toward life and the world. When I was younger, I had experienced what seemed like more than my fair share of disappointments. Things that were promised never seemed to materialize, and I got into the habit of believing that good things would never happen to me. Imagining the worst-case scenario, I thought, was a surefire way of avoiding disappointment. What I discovered later was that believing the worst also left me a miserable and depressed person.

> Imagining the worst-case scenario, I thought, was a surefire way of avoiding disappointment. What I discovered later was that believing the worst also left me a miserable and depressed person.

It has taken time for that to change. As we gaze at heaven and then take our eyes and place them on the world, heaven affects our vision—Son blindness, if you like. It affects the way we see our lives. Now I believe that God has a plan for my life, that He knows, loves and will look after me. My life may not be pain free, but ultimately, God is in charge, and I'm going to see Him face-to-face.

Whatever your situation, as you worship God, you will be set free.

HOW DOES GOD SET YOU FREE?

It works like this: As we look at God, seeking a vision of heaven, we get His perspective on the world. Jesus said, "If you hold to my teaching, you are really my disciples. Then you will know the truth, and the truth shall set you free" (John 8:32).

One of the ideas Jesus was alluding to was that in knowing the truth, we get to know Him—after all, He is the way, the truth and the life (see John 14:6). And also, we begin to absorb more of God's truth. The falsehoods in our lives are exposed, and through worship of a loving, majestic God, we realize that His loving-kindness does endure forever. We gradually begin to believe it, and we move from earthbound untruths to heaven-inspired absolutes.

When we see that the God we worship is the creator of the entire universe, even when things don't go so well for us, then problems and disappointments no longer seem quite so bad. After all, since He is the ultimate boss, who are we to argue when He seems to take things in a slightly different direction from the one we had in mind?

For example, when something bad happened to Joseph—like being sold into slavery by his brothers—he decided not to get bitter. He told his brothers years later that what they meant for harm, God meant for good. "God sent me ahead of you . . . to save your lives by a great deliverance," Joseph said to his brothers (Gen. 45:7). If Joseph had refused to forgive his brothers, then all his claims about God's greatness, all his worship and devotion, would have meant nothing. If we are to have integrity, if our worship is to have integrity, then it must spill over to the attitudes of our lives.

We Christians have often been on the receiving end of the criticism that we can be too focused on heaven to be of any earthly use. I think the same can be said the other way around: that we can also be too focused on the things of Earth to be any heavenly use. When we are focused on heaven in the best way, then we are fit for a life on Earth. It helps when we see things the right way around, get things in the right order and realize our place in the universe.

Note

1. Matt Redman, "I Will Offer Up My Life" (Eastbourne, UK: Kingsway's Thankyou Music, 1994).

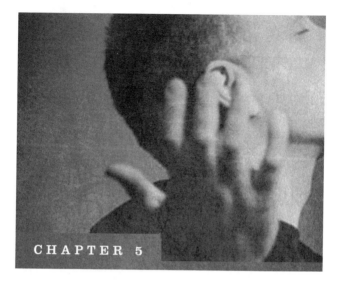

CHAPTER 5

THE FRUIT OF WORSHIP: PART 2—HOLINESS

I used to be more of a man than I am today. In fact, at one point, there was about one-third more to Mike Pilavachi—and most of it was the human equivalent of an airbag. In short, I was cuddly (so long as you had very long arms). In my fat-free year that was 1998, I grilled and steamed my way through mountains of fish and vegetables, and panted across numerous virtual miles on my treadmill. I became so obsessed with the fat content of food that my prayer life began to take on a distinctly dietary flavor. "Oh, Lord," I would pipe up in church, "restrict our intake of harmful sin, and raise our metabolic rate so that we too may deliver new converts faster than a bowl of pure fiber." People soon got the message.

While I was changing on the outside, I was hoping that I might get a "two for one" deal and change on the inside also. I hoped that, by way of reward for all my hard work, God might give my soul a little tweak and make me into a holier Christian. Unfortunately that wasn't to be, and at the end of the year I had to content myself with a very large collection of very large trousers.

What I did discover was that while hard work and discipline can do wonders for the gut, on their own they do very little for the soul. I was hoping that I could work my way into God's good books, that a little spiritual sweat would deliver the goods. Eventually I saw the light, and realized that sanctification (a technical word that means to be made holy), like salvation, has nothing to do with our hard work, and everything to do with God's mighty grace. We can see this revelation plastered throughout the four Gospels—ask yourself who, from prostitutes to tax collectors, actually deserved Jesus' time, let alone

His healing? Sanctification is a gift from God. In the same way that Jesus bought our forgiveness by offering Himself as a sacrifice on the cross, He lets us hitch a ride and approach God, as He becomes our holiness.

True holiness is so much more than self-discipline. Repeating a list of "must not's" (I must not be jealous, I must not be angry, I must not get bitter, and so on) is not the way to bring about the desired results (unless, of course, the desired result is that you lose both your sanity and your friends). Even at our best, we could never match up to Christ's standards of holiness. It therefore makes sense to ask Jesus to make us more holy by His power, not by our own.

"HOLINESS" IN THE BIBLE

With a little detective work, it soon becomes clear that the Bible contains much on this subject of holiness. In fact, in Colossians, Paul tempts us with the declaration that he is about to reveal the secret that has been hidden through the ages. Apparently, this particular secret was to be kept hidden from people until Christ had died and risen. Paul is the one charged with the task of revealing the mystery, and he drops the bomb in Colossians 1:27, where he writes, "Christ in you, the hope of glory."

Excuse me? Is that it—the secret that was hidden for so long? "Christ in you, the hope of glory"? It doesn't make sense, does it? But take out the word "you" and replace it with your name, and swap the word "hope" for "prospect." Imagine it's an election campaign slogan, and it starts to make sense: "Christ in Mike, the prospect of glory." With Jesus in my life, there is a chance of things being better, of my being more holy, of final glory.

Things become even clearer when you check out some more of Paul's letters. Turn to Galatians 2:20, and read as he expands the ideas of our powerlessness to change ourselves and of our reliance on Him. "I have been crucified with Christ," Paul writes, "it is no longer I who live but Christ who lives in me." That's exactly what it means to have Christ living in us, by His Spirit. In the same way that God's incarnation involved His becoming human flesh, so too has Jesus become incarnated in the Body of Christ, the Church. As Christians and members of the Body, we have the chance to be intimately involved with Him through the Church and through our relationship with Him. We are meant to be a people of His presence; we are supposed to interact with our Maker, to have Him at the center of our lives.

The Place of Worship

Before I send off hoards of people thinking that God hands out holiness to all and sundry like a senile Santa at Christmas, perhaps I ought to set the record straight. Remember, this is in the context of worship—it comes when we have relationship with God.

Worship is central to this whole process. If we are really going to get to grips with our ambition to become more holy, more like our Savior, then we simply must devote ourselves to worship.

It's a well-known fact that people are often influenced by their surroundings. I pick up accents faster than I used to pick up a cream cake, and whenever I visit South Africa, I return having adopted a nasal quality to my voice and a batch of stock phrases such as "Yeah, yeah" and "See you just now." When people finally understand what I'm saying, they often think I'm mimicking them on purpose, but the truth is that I simply can't help it. So connect the dots here: If you start thinking or sounding a bit like the people you hang out with, how much more will time spent with the Lord our God produce desirable side effects? So how do we hang out with the Lord? We hang out with Him primarily through worship and intimate relationship.

Paul's second letter to the Corinthians supports the idea that being with Him is to become like Him. It says, "Now the Lord is the Spirit, and where the Spirit of the Lord is, there is freedom. And we, who with unveiled faces all reflect the Lord's glory, are being transformed into his likeness with ever-increasing glory, which comes from the Lord, who is the Spirit" (2 Cor. 3:17-18).

This pivotal verse about holiness deserves some unpacking. Paul had just been writing about Moses and pointing out how, after Moses had been up the mountain and seen God face-to-face, he had to cover his face with a veil since it shone so much. After a short time, the radiance that was covered by the veil began to fade away. Simply being in God's presence was enough for Moses to come away from the meeting with something of God left on him. In the same way then, we should expect to be transformed when we spend time with the Lord. Through the death of Jesus, a new covenant has been established, a new promise that encourages us to spend as much time with Him as possible.

The key to this idea can be found in the word that has been translated as "reflect," which can also be taken to mean "contemplate."[1] The translators obviously had a little bit of a disagreement over this one and apparently the "reflect" team won. It's good to see that those "contemplate" boys didn't go down without a fight though, as their little addition opens up the entire text of 2 Corinthians 3:17-18. The reason for their dilemma was that the actual Greek phrase that they were translating supported both interpretations. While "reflect" and "contemplate" seem to be on different sides of the camp when it comes to meaning, the translators discovered that the original Greek word was linked to the act of looking into a mirror. When looking in a mirror, we both reflect and contemplate what we see before us: We provide the mirror with an image to reflect, we take a moment to think about our personal appearance and we get the chance to see a little bit of who we are. The original text carries the idea that as we look at the Lord, we will both understand more of Him and take on more of His qualities.

This is the same idea as when you hang out with

someone a lot and you start taking on his or her characteristics, especially if it is someone you love. It is a constant source of amazement how many adopted kids I meet who in many ways resemble their adoptive parents, although genetically they are nothing like them. Somehow just being with them sparks

> **The good news is that being a Christian is not about attempting to pay God back by trying to be like Him; it's about letting Him be God in our lives.**

an internal change, which can be visible on the surface. The same is true with Jesus: The more we look at Him, the more we look like Him, and the more His character rubs off on ours.

This is an incredibly potent encouragement for us as Christians. If we want to become more like Jesus, the solution is neither navel gazing nor apathy; it won't come by sitting around waiting for God to get around to us when He has time, nor will it come by our trying to force out the fruit of the Spirit. The good news is that being a Christian is not about attempting to pay God back by trying to be like Him; it's about letting Him be God in our lives. That means giving Him time, space and respect. I have to let His character grow in me, and I can do that by hanging out with Him. I have to look at and study Him in order to reflect Him. That's how worship is central to the Christian life. Without worship, we have no relationship with our God, and there is little chance of our being transformed into His likeness. If I want to become more holy, let me spend a few hours worshiping and I will walk away with something of the shine on my face that Moses experienced. I haven't got to the stage of needing a veil yet, but I'm sure I've changed inside.

THE FRUIT OF WORSHIP

The fruit of the Spirit as described in Galatians 5:22-23 is set up as the primary aim for us Christians. When combined, the collection of qualities that make up the fruit of the Spirit, form a perfect description of Jesus Himself. Bearing in mind Paul's words about being "transformed" through worship (2 Cor. 3:18), it seems that these character improvements aren't as hard to develop as we may have first thought. Someone said once that we shouldn't pray, "Lord give me joy, love and patience," but we should say, "Lord, I want more of You in me." Why wear ourselves out by trying desperately to improve our levels of self-control when we can get the whole package by being transformed into His likeness?

The concept of Christ living within us can seem strange and almost unnatural. Paul used the same phrases to illustrate an intimacy with and a radical commitment to his Creator. Let us return to Galatians 2:20 where Paul says, "I have been crucified with Christ and I no longer live, but Christ lives in me." The more we look at Him, the more His character and His personality begin to be lived out in us. That is something that only Jesus can do, and it is one of the fruits of worship, something that takes time.

We've mentioned the fruit of the Spirit, and it is important to note that it is the Spirit's fruit, not ours. Going a little further with this idea, we know that fruit trees aren't exactly flexible when it comes down to production; a pear tree won't produce apples any more than a banana tree will produce strawberries. No amount of concentration, hard work or fertilizer will help either tree divert from its genetic script. The fruit of the Spirit is a description of the character of Jesus, and the only person who can bear the fruit of the Spirit is Jesus.

What is more, you don't see many fruit trees getting all stressed when it comes round to delivering the goods; the process is as natural as can be. Only Jesus can tease out the characteristics of love, joy, peace, patience, kindness, goodness, gentleness, humility and self-control. And it comes naturally to Him.

Another problem that I used to encounter in the whole fruit arena was that I wanted my spiritual development to be instantaneous. "Give me more patience," I once demanded of the Lord, "now." But growing fruit always takes a full season. You cannot expect the apples to be hours away as soon as the blossom arrives; instead, you need to allow the development to take place over the months and years. Once the period of basking in the summer sun is over, the apples tend to be ready, but only then.

I used to examine myself regularly for fruit growth. Were my anger levels subsiding? How was that baby shoot of patience I first noticed last week? Had the love taken root yet? It was only when someone pointed out to me that the trees themselves don't tend to get much in the way of gratification when they produce fruit that I realized where I had been going wrong. The fruit of the Spirit—the by-products of our worship—are not there to be measured by us; they aren't even there for us. Instead, they are there for the benefit of those around us.

All this fruit imagery is basic stuff, but in a way I think that we need to be reminded of just how fundamental the truth of all this is: If we spend time with God, we grow closer to Him. Straight after Paul's bit about unveiled faces, we are offered some further thoughts on holiness:

> But we have this treasure in jars of clay to show that this all-surpassing power is from God and not from us. We are hard pressed on every side, but not crushed; perplexed, but not in despair; persecuted, but not abandoned; struck down, but not destroyed. We always carry around in our body the death of Jesus, so that the life of Jesus may also be revealed in our body (2 Cor. 4:7-10).

Sometimes we have our brains set to the wrong frequency and we end up misinterpreting so many things. We get confused about the fruit of the Spirit, and we get it all wrong about victory, glory and holiness. The truth is that we will always be the jars of clay and God will always be the treasure.

Let me explain. Paul's analogy was particularly relevant to his audience at the time. In the first century there were no banks and there were no safety deposit boxes. Anything of worth had to be looked after by the owner. The more prosperous folk, those who wanted to keep something of value for their old age or to pass on when they died, would look for suitable hiding places in their own homes. Obviously, one of the places that would have been way down on any list of top hiding places would have been a valuable vase. You can imagine the scenario: thief steals the vase and unwittingly gets the fancy jewelry too. He's very happy; the owner's very sad. So what the rich people used to do in those days—and it actually became well known, so I'm surprised that the thieves didn't figure it out—was to get ordinary clay pots and use them as hiding places for their most valuable possessions.

You know, it's the same with us: We're jars of clay. We're not great ornamental vases. We're jars of clay, broken pots. Many of us are broken pots in which God has chosen to put His treasure, the treasure of His life and the treasure of the life of His Son. He puts it in my jar of clay, and that is the secret of the Christian faith. It is not my being something that I am not; it is Jesus being who He is through me. This is what radiates life.

Immediately after talking about treasure in jars of clay, Paul says, "We are hard pressed on every side, but not crushed; perplexed, but not in despair." It's wonderful because it's a twofold thing—I find Him in the midst of my weakness.

According to Paul, God sees us this way too. We're unworthy, yet He still trusts us with His treasure. Paul explains how it works. We are hard pressed on every side but not crushed. We are "perplexed, but not in despair." That feels like an accurate description of me throughout most of my life: perplexed but not quite in despair. I used to think that it is wrong to be perplexed, that true faith has no room for doubt. To find Paul saying "perplexed, but not in despair; persecuted, but not abandoned; struck down, but not destroyed" was a fantastic relief. We don't have to pretend to be something we're not; we can approach God in our weakness and pain. How does this apply to worship? It applies because we are meant to come to God in worship with all our pains and frustrations, without holding anything back.

There's that wonderful place in the Bible where Paul says, "There was given me a thorn in my flesh, a messenger of Satan, to torment me. Three times I pleaded with the Lord to take it from me. But he said to me, 'My grace is sufficient for you, for my power is made perfect in weakness'" (2 Cor. 12:7-9). Whatever that thorn in the flesh was (perhaps a physical problem like his eyesight or a relationship problem that couldn't get healed—some people even speculate that it was with his wife, though the Bible doesn't confirm that Paul was ever married), the point is that there was something Paul struggled with. The point is that Paul was a jar of clay, and like us, there was no need for him to be ashamed of his weakness.

Note

1. Walter Bauer, William F. Arndt and F. Wilbur Gingrich, *A Greek-Enlish Lexicon of the New Testament and Other Early Christian Literature*, 2nd ed., (Chicago: University of Chicago Press, 1979), s.v. "katopridzo," p. 424d.

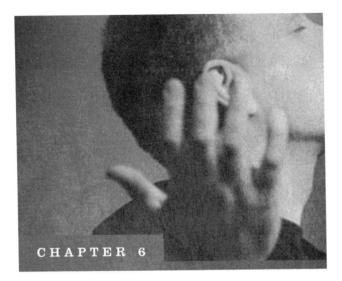

CHAPTER 6

PROPHETIC INTERCESSION

This is my dream: I'm standing in a crowded bus station, with people on all sides straining to see the buses as they pull up in front of us. Everyone is either whistling or humming, causing the station to echo with an eerie sonic song. As the buses pull in, they let off all their passengers. None of these travelers are whistling or humming. Instead, they all look exhausted. They fall to the floor and sleep. In time they get up—revived by their rest—and begin to join in the chorus with their own whistled or hummed tunes. No one ever gets on the bus; instead, the crowd seems more intent on catching the drivers' eyes as they arrive. Often the drivers seem tired, but the noise and atmosphere in the depot spur them on. They seem to get recharged more quickly than their beleaguered passengers, and before long they drive their buses back out of the station. Now put this series of images on the back burner until the end of the chapter.

HONEST WORSHIP

There are times when we aren't totally honest with God in our worship. Some of us have been guilty of being bogus worship junkies, desperate to lose ourselves in an hour of exuberant worship to wash away the cares of a busy week. Surely, half a dozen happy worship songs sung back-to-back as a pick-me-up isn't quite the way that worship of the almighty God is supposed to be. Surely, our worship should not be a means of escape from the world. If the psalms are anything to go by, worship is supposed to be an opportunity to express the depth of our hearts to God.

Psalm 42 starts (as do quite a number of David's other psalms) with a declaration that David's enemies have him surrounded, that God has abandoned him and that his tears flow throughout the night. Yet, the chapter ends with "for I will yet praise him, my Savior and my God." It seems that in the Church we are very good at getting on with the rejoicing bits, but not so good at expressing the despair.

I was challenged on this when I visited Graham Cray in Cambridge. Graham is Principal of Ridley Hall, Cambridge, a theological college and pastor factory. Occasionally, Matt Redman and I go up to visit him and talk. One particular time, I asked Graham where he thought our worship was going wrong. Thinking quietly to myself, *Go ahead, have a swipe at Redman*, I sat back and waited for Graham's answer. He was very gracious and he started off saying to Matt, "Well, I love your songs; they are so Christ-centered." Then he said, "As you ask, the thing that I've always been wondering is generally, where is the place for lament in our worship?" Lament? I was confused. He pointed to the psalms, the songs of exile, the songs about sitting down and weeping by the rivers of Babylon. All we do, he suggested, is sing the happy bits, the "I will praise you, rejoice in you at all times" bits.

I must admit to feeling sorry for the poor chap;

too much theology had obviously affected his perception. "Graham," I patronized, "you must not realize that we're not in exile any more. We don't need to sing songs of lament because Jesus died on the cross, remember, and brought us home. We are now His people; we are Christians." I sat back and waited for him to catch on.

"Who told you that?" he replied.

I looked confused.

"Who told you that we were no longer in exile?" Graham said. "Who said there are no laments to be sung to God? Are we really at home, with all the pain, turmoil, killings and hatred in the world? Is there nothing to lament about before God? Is there nothing to cry out? Is there no intercession we can make in our worship? And even if we can't sing songs of lament in our worship for ourselves, surely we ought to be bringing to God the pain of the world in our worship."

What had we missed? We had ignored the value of intercession, the power of bringing the imperfections of the world before God and asking Him to move.

Having said that, on one level we don't want to go too far down that road, because God is ultimately good, whether we feel like it or not. We need to remember to maintain a sense of balance in our worship. Like David and the psalmists, we need to be brutally honest with God about the things that trouble us, as well as acknowledge His goodness and power. At times we may not feel at all like worshiping, and it is at those times that it is most important that we get on with the business of exercising our faith. That's worshiping in the midst of reality, and worship is supposed to reflect life.

> Like David and the psalmists, we need to be able to be brutally honest with God about the things that trouble us, as well as to be able to acknowledge His goodness and power.

And so we come to the practical challenge of working out how we can worship God and remain 100 percent honest and faithful. How do we marry pain with praise? I think we've got a lot of work to do on that. At Soul Survivor Watford, we've been trying to explore this ground—or at least endeavoring to understand it a little more, even if we haven't quite found a solution yet. When we have tried to learn about intercession in worship, fresh songs have arrived, and many of the songs have captured the spirit of the time. But I think we've got a long way to go to ensure that worship remains God-centered while we express our questions.

I have a strange feeling that we can learn much on this topic from the period in David's life after he killed Uriah the Hittite, Bathsheba's husband (after David had slept with her) (see 2 Sam. 11). The Lord sent the prophet Nathan to David to ask what he had done. David repented bitterly. Later, his child, born as a result of the affair, became ill, and the Lord said he was going to take him from David. David spent days weeping, mourning and refusing to eat. He called out to God in intercession; and when the boy died, the servants didn't know how to tell him, because they were worried about his reaction. David saw them talking and asked the servants if the boy had died. "He has, my Lord," they answered. With that, David washed his face, got dressed and went to worship. As the servants stared on in disbelief, David explained that there was no point in mourning any longer; God's will had been done (2 Sam. 12).

Depending on your point of view, David's reaction is, at first glance, either commendable or contemptible. Throughout the passage, David continually placed himself in a position of submission, affirming to God that He was in control. He knew that God's decision would be final and, perhaps more important, that it would be just. Despite the pain and sorrow it caused him, David was willing to trust God and accept His decision. As soon as his son died, David was back worshiping God. There was no bitterness; there were no recriminations; there were just supplication and trust. David must have worshiped with a broken heart; the weeping and mourning were certainly not part of a show. Since there was a place for David to worship God in his despair, then surely it must be worth our while to worship in the midst of our own dark times.

During that first conversation in Cambridge, Graham talked about how as God's people, we need to be saying, "Oh, God, where are You?" Even if we are not doing that for our own situations, we should be doing it on behalf of a hurt and broken world. When it comes to worship, how self-indulgent it is for us to come and say, "Forget everything out there; let's just sing our happy songs." How dare we keep it all for ourselves! When we come to worship, of course we need to rejoice, to praise and to give thanks, but we also need to make space to bring our intercessions and our songs of lament.

In the psalms of lament there is an "I'm going to be honest about how I feel about this" attitude. Psalm 77 carries that sentiment throughout, and the psalmist writes, "Will the Lord reject forever? Will he never show his favor again?" (v. 7).

Sometimes our worship is too much like a quick fix. In search of my own quick fixes of escapism, junk food and sun, I went to California, the home of "the happiest place on Earth." Walk through Disneyland's gates and suddenly you are in a land of magic and joy, where you can forget the cares you had at home. Everything there is so bright and fluffy and wonderful. Mickey's smiling, and that's all that counts. Never having been there before, I was surprised at the sense of déjà vu that settled in my head. Then I realized that Disneyland was just like the church. Sometimes we come through the church's doors and think it is a place where we can forget the cares of the world. All those problems and pains are whisked away in a soufflé of happy lives and well-pressed clothes. It doesn't matter that our hearts are breaking; gloss it over with a few fast songs, and reality need never be an issue. That's wrong. When we come in worship, we come with all that we are and all that we have—if we gloss, squash or numb any part, then our worship is fake. Worship is bringing who we are to Him; worship should be an expression of life.

The Hebrews didn't suffer quite so badly in this area. They didn't divide life into the sacred and the secular, into the things of the world and the things of the Spirit. That attitude is the legacy of Greek philosophy, inspired by Plato and his pals. The Sunday Christian attitude, in which one acts like a Christian only once a week, is simply not a biblical concept. One of the words that is used in the Old Testament for "worship" literally means "to work."[1] That isn't a reference to working in the Temple or to working in the Church; it just means "to work." That's right, they saw room for worship in the middle of farming, fixing and creating. Applied to today's job market, worship can be expressed through the medium of anything from recruitment consulting to hairdressing. For the Jewish people, their understanding was that the whole of life should be an act of worship. So whether we are an industry fat cat or a blue-collar underling, worship is a celebration of life, a communication and a communion with God.

That's why Jewish culture valued the tearing of clothes as an act of worship as much as the banging of a tambourine. In the U.K., the Church still bangs the tambourines, but we seem to have stopped tearing our clothes. The expressions of sorrow must be reintroduced into our communion with God, as they are part of the blueprint of our souls. Who would dream of chastising a parent mourning the loss of a teenage son? But when did we last sing a song that would be of real help in that kind of situation? True, God's light does transcend pain, it does shine in the darkness, but it also illuminates the pain of the Cross. It is good for us to say, "for I will yet praise him, my Savior and my God"; but that "yet" can only really come after we have told the Lord exactly where we are. That is faith. It's about coming to Him in reality. It's praising Him through the tears, not pretending that the tears aren't there.

If prophecy reveals whatever is on God's heart, then you can be pretty sure that God's heart is, among other things, in mourning for all those who don't have a relationship with Him. After all, didn't Jesus put evangelism at the top of our to-do list before He went back to heaven? Worship is a two-way process: We hang out with God, and we are transformed by His very nature. It therefore seems clear that our worship is missing something if we don't step in line with God's attitudes toward all people. Worship and prayer can become fused here, both being used to bend God's ear on behalf of our neighbors.

PICTURES OF PROPHETIC INTERCESSION

Since Graham put us back on course, different songs have come up through Soul Survivor that helped us truly express how we feel through worship. The titles of the songs hint at this tendency ("Can a Nation Be Changed?" and "Knocking on the Door of Heaven," to name two).

Prophetic intercession, I believe, is an aspect of worship. It should come out of a lifestyle of worship in the same way that the Hebrews found their everyday lives to be incredibly compatible with their faith. There is a story in Ezekiel 4 that teaches us in an unusual way what prophetic intercession is all about. In this story, the Lord told Ezekiel, "Now, son of man, take a clay tablet, put it in front of you and draw the city of Jerusalem on it" (v. 1). So he drew.

There's the Temple, there are some houses, there's the mountain, there are some clouds in the sky, and there's a little bit of grass there. "Then lay siege to it: Erect siege works against it, build a ramp up to it, set up camps against it and put battering rams around it" (v. 2). Then he had to get a little model war going, make battering rams and a ramp, and find something to represent the soldiers. It appears that this was not in the privacy of his back room. We're talking 100 percent public.

"Hello, Ezekiel. What are you doing?" his neighbors may have asked him.

"I'm drawing the city of Jerusalem on this clay tablet."

"What are you doing now, Ezekiel?"

"I'm laying siege to Jerusalem. I have built my battering rams."

"I can see that."

"And here's my ramp and my siege works and my soldiers."

"That's nice, Ezekiel."

Then in verse 3 of chapter 4 the Lord said, "Then, take an iron pan and place it as an iron wall between you and the city and turn your face towards it. It will be under siege, and you shall besiege it. This will be a sign to the house of Israel." If you want my opinion that was a sign that Ezekiel had finally gone foot-chewingly mad. But it gets worse, because then he gets into the real nutty stuff.

> Then lie on your left side and put the sin of the house of Israel upon yourself. You are to bear their sin for the number of days that you lie on your side. I have assigned you the same number of days as the years of their sin. So for 390 days you will bear the sin of the house of Israel (vv. 4-5).

Now, let's make sure we understand this next bit. God told Ezekiel to lie on his side: "Lie down in front of the clay tablet with Jerusalem on it, with the siege works. Lie down and put the sin of Israel on you. Right, now you're to lie there in front of Jerusalem for one day for every year of Israel's sin: 390 days, representing 390 years." So Ezekiel lay on his left side in front of the clay tablet for 390 days. That's over a year. That's a very long time. He missed Christmas and his birthday too. Again, the neighbors probably would have come by.

"Hello, Ezekiel. What are you doing?"

"Ah, I'm lying in front of the city of Jerusalem."

"But you were besieging it yesterday."

"Yes, well, today I am lying in front of it and the sin of Israel is upon me."

"Oh."

"Yes, and I'll be here for another year."

And then he had to lay on his other side for the number of days that Judah had sinned in years, which was another 40 days. And when he was done that for 390 days plus 40 days, the Lord said, "Turn your face toward the siege of Jerusalem and with bared arm prophesy against her" (v. 7). Now what does that mean? Jerusalem was under siege from her enemies, and God set Ezekiel up for a prophetic act. There can be real drama in prophecy, and this is Oscar material. We are told that he stood with bared arm and prophesied against Jerusalem. Can you imagine the pain he must have felt after having laid on his arm for 390 days? Now, exactly how much of this story is symbolic, I don't know; but we take it, for teaching purposes, at face value.

So I think that as Ezekiel spoke, he wouldn't have opted for the soft and gentle approach, the one that goes, "Well, Israel, you have been naughty boys and girls, haven't you? The Lord said He's not very pleased. You'd best do better next time." And "Oh, well, I've done that prophecy now. I'd best go on to the next place."

I don't think he did that. I think that after lying there for 390 days, when he lifted up his arm in agony, he didn't just say what God's asked him to. Instead he prophesied God's heart; he actually felt some of God's pain. That is what prophetic intercession is all about, and it's part of worship.

Another example of how prophetic intercession reveals the heart and pain of God can be found in the story of Hosea. God told Hosea to take the prostitute Gomer as his wife. God also told him that she would be unfaithful to him, but that Hosea was to love, care for and treasure her as he would the most faithful of wives (see Hosea 1). Once this had gone according to plan, God told Hosea to go and say to Israel, "Israel is corrupt. Their deeds do not permit them to return to God. A spirit of prostitution is in their heart, they do not acknowledge the Lord" (Hosea 5:3-4).

When Hosea prophesied, even expert theologians find it hard to tell, studying the book of Hosea, which part was Hosea speaking and which part was God. This prophecy is so powerful, because Hosea was actually living the suffering that God felt. God told Hosea to take this prostitute so that when he prophesied over Israel, the words would have maximum force. When Hosea spoke, it was both a spiritual revelation.

I'll never forget this story that John Wimber told years ago. He was speaking at a camp when a pastor friend of his told him that there was a woman in the church who said she had a prophecy for him. John said to his friend, "Yeah, right. She's probably just single, in her late forties and in need of affirmation." His friend replied that she was all of those things, but she also was usually pretty good at hearing God. So when the woman came up to John, he said, "Well, lady, go on. I hear you have a prophecy for me." The woman burst into tears and started crying. John Wimber thought, *Oh no, here we go, I've got an emotional female here.* After a while he got fed up and said, "Listen, lady, I'm a busy man. I don't know what your problem is, but can you tell me the prophecy and then we can get going." She was sobbing her heart out. Then she looked up at him through her tears and said, "That's the prophecy." It was as though a knife had gone through John's heart, because suddenly he saw that God was crying over him. God was brokenhearted over him, over his sin, over his brokenness, over his pride and over his arrogance. He said that he walked into the woods and cried back. A woman's tears changed his life, but they were God's tears.

When Hosea spoke to Israel about how they had prostituted themselves to every passing god, his agony was God's agony and it spoke to Israel. When Ezekiel bared his arm, he felt God's pain. Sometimes God uses us in ways that we might not understand. Our logical brains can shield us from revelation. Our hearts are often not so well defended. It is from there

> **When Hosea spoke to Israel about how they had prostituted themselves to every passing god, his agony was God's agony and it spoke to Israel.**

that intercession comes. Don't get me wrong—there is a real value in quietly working through a list of people and situations in need of prayer. There is also a place for being doubled over on the floor, aching for God to do something. As it says in Romans 8:26, "We do not know what we ought to pray for, but the

Spirit himself intercedes for us with sighs and groans too deep for words." Intercession can often take the form of sighs and groans too deep for words. Words are important, but they are not the only way.

In our church in Watford, we haven't learned very much about this yet, and I don't always know how to get there; but even as I write this, I am thinking that we have got to find a way. We have our praise and thanksgiving—both precious things—but we also have our intercession, in which we share something of God's heart and we allow Him to break our hearts with the things that break His. That's biblical worship, and I believe that the closer we get to Jesus in and through our worship, the more we will feel His pain.

It's a funny thing, but have you ever noticed how good we have become at covering up our pain? How the shock of sudden negative emotions can lead to a knee-jerk reaction of suppression and denial? We're not good with pain—after all, who wants to hang out with someone who is permanently miserable? But when we do that repression thing, we also succeed in taking the edge off those decent emotions like joy and happiness. The people that I know who are truly alive are the ones who are willing to embrace the pain as well as the joy.

When you care a lot for people, you can't feel great joy when you see them without feeling great sorrow when they're gone. This happens in our worship too. While we have the great joy of knowing Jesus, He'll also break our hearts; He'll melt our hearts so that we sense something of His pain for this hurting and broken world. That's why I love some of Kevin Prosch's songs—they're honest. In his song "Break Our Hearts," Kevin writes, "Oh, break our hearts with the things that break yours."[2] What a line.

Another great song of Kevin's is "How Can I Be Satisfied?" The chorus carries the lines "How can I be satisfied, unless you come near and stay by my side? There has to be more, Lord, there must be more."[3] Some people have said that this should not be sung in worship, because feeling far from God is not something to complain to God about; it's not His fault. While I understand this, the psalms also have a recurring theme of "where are You, Lord?" Whatever the reason, I want the Lord to hear my cry for this world.

This is where worship, intercession and my dream all come together. The dream I described in the beginning of this chapter is about standing on the sidelines, watching as the lost are brought in. While we are not the bearers of salvation, I think we should play a big part in this picture. Our worship can be that part. As we evangelize, lament and intercede in our worship, somehow we can find a way of pulling it all together.

Notes

1. *Strong's Exhaustive Concordance of the Bible*, # 5647, s.v. "abad."
2. Kevin Prosch, "Break Our Hearts," *Reckless Mercy* (Vertical Music, 1998).
3. Kevin Prosch, "How Can I Be Satisfied," *Come to the Light* (7th Time Music, 1993).

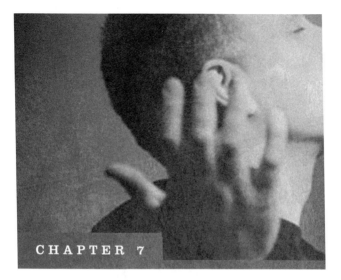

CHAPTER 7

WORSHIP AND SPIRITUAL WARFARE

One of the devil's major strategies is to deflect our attention from God and put it onto himself. It makes sense, doesn't it, that he would want to try to sever the link that exists between God and His creation? Assuming that, it makes sense that the greatest antidote that we have in our possession is worship. By going deeper with God, we counteract the devil's attempts to distract us. I also believe that when we worship, battles are won in the heavenly places.

Things get changed when we worship. Jesus said He came to proclaim and usher in the Kingdom. The devil will do all he can to prevent the rule of God on Earth. When we worship, we acknowledge the King of the Kingdom; and as we do, the dynamic rule of God advances. Worship is the supreme weapon of our warfare. It is the Christian's nuclear bomb.

Now we're going to look at the story of King Jehoshaphat, as told in 2 Chronicles 20.

Some men came and told Jehoshaphat, "A vast army is coming against you from Edom, from the other side of the Sea. It is already in Hazazon Tamar" (that is, En Gedi). Alarmed, Jehoshaphat resolved to inquire of the Lord, and he proclaimed a fast for all of Judah. The people of Judah came together to seek help from the Lord; indeed, they came from every town in Judah to seek him (vv. 2-4).

This reaction to the threat of attack, this unanimous decision to fall to their knees, is one of the most inspired examples of faith and humility in the Old Testament. And sure enough, it paid off: "Then the Spirit of the Lord came upon Jahaziel son of

Zechariah, the son of Benaiah, the son of Jeiel, the son of Mattaniah, a Levite and descendant of Asaph, as he stood in the assembly" (v. 14).

Notice the attention to the family history. This history is there to add a little color to the characters, but it also sheds some important biographical light on the proceedings. Jahaziel's great, great, great grandfather was a Levite, which means that he was a priest—the equivalent of a modern-day worship leader. Asaph was one of the most famous worship leaders in all of Israel. He was around at the time of King David, and it seems like he passed something down through the generations.

In verse 15 Jahaziel begins to speak:

Listen, King Jehoshaphat and all who live in Judah and Jerusalem! This is what the Lord says to you: "Do not be afraid or discouraged because of this vast army. For the battle is not yours, but God's. Tomorrow march down against them. They will be climbing up by the Pass of Ziz, and you will find them at the end of the gorge in the Desert of Jeruel. You will not have to fight this battle. Take up your positions; stand firm and see

the deliverance the Lord will give you, O
Judah and Jerusalem. Do not be afraid; do
not be discouraged. Go out to face them
tomorrow, and the Lord will be with you"
(2 Chron. 20:15-17).

When you think about it, that is an amazing statement. There were three armies rolled into one vast
enemy. They seemed huge and were practically guar-
anteed to wipe the floor with Jehoshaphat's crew. But
what does the Lord say? "Relax—it's not your battle."

I know how I have would responded to such
strange advice, and it would not be the way
Jehoshaphat responded in verse 18: "Jehoshaphat
bowed with his face to the ground, and all the people
of Judah and Jerusalem fell down in worship before
the Lord." I give Jehoshaphat points for that reaction. It sparked more of the same from others gath-
ered around, and some Levites from the Kohathites
and Korahites stood up and praised the Lord, the
God of Israel, with a loud voice.

The story goes on:

Early in the morning they left for the Desert
of Tekoa. As they set out, Jehoshaphat stood

and said, "Listen to me, Judah and people of Jerusalem! Have faith in the Lord your God and you will be upheld; have faith in his prophets and you will be successful." After consulting the people, Jehoshaphat appointed men to sing to the Lord and to praise him for the splendor of his holiness as they went out at the head of the army, saying: "Give thanks to the Lord, for his love endures forever" (vv. 20-21).

What happened? Jehoshaphat put worshipers at the forefront of his army. The men were there to praise God for the splendor of His holiness so that as the army went out to fight, the battle really would be God's. They praised God by singing, "Give thanks to the Lord, for his love endures forever."

Then we read verse 22: "As they began to sing and praise, the Lord set ambushes against the men of Ammon and Moab and Mount Seir who were invading Judah, and they were defeated." While Israel worshiped, God won the battle. It turns out that the enemies fought among themselves to the extent that "When the men of Judah came to the place that overlooks the desert and looked toward the vast army, they saw only dead bodies lying on the ground; no one had escaped" (v. 24).

> **When we think that our enemies or our circumstances are like vast armies aligned against us, the greatest weapon we have is worship.**

Sometimes when things are tough, when we don't know what else to do, we think that our enemies or our circumstances are like vast armies aligned against us. At those times the greatest weapon we have is worship. Praising God in the midst of our difficulties, saying to Him that we believe the battle is His rather than ours, can be the catalyst for true signs and wonders. The deal for us is the same as that which God offered Jehoshaphat: We worship and He fights.

We see the same principle at work in the book of Acts, when Paul and Silas were jailed at Philippi. They had been arrested and put into prison, held in chains in the deepest dungeon. At midnight, instead of sleeping or complaining or trying to escape, they worshiped God. At that time, an earthquake just happened to be brewing; and as it rattled the prison, their door flew open and their chains fell off. The good stuff didn't just stop there, because the jailer and his family all came to know Jesus. With God fighting the battle, they had no need to implement any of their own strategies. Worship was enough; God did the rest.

In this context, worship and praise can build faith. When we look solely at the circumstances that are worrying us, we can find ourselves overwhelmed. But when we give thanks and recount the reasons why we can be thankful to God, our faith is built and we begin to believe what we are saying.

There are many Christians who seem to be locked up in prisons of their own making. If only they would turn to worship and praise instead of focusing on their problems, then their prison doors would open and their chains would fall away. We need to use praise as a spiritual weapon against the enemy. It is so much healthier than spending time talking to the enemy, rebuking him and telling him off. We want to put our attention where it belongs—Jesus Christ.

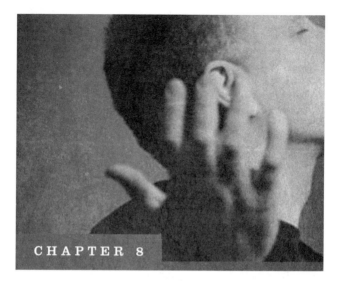

CHAPTER 8

CREATIVITY IN WORSHIP

The very first thing we know about God from Genesis 1 is that He likes to create. Having figured that one out, it becomes clear that we too, being made in His image, have a natural desire and ability to create, reflecting the nature of our Maker.

From these observations, it doesn't take a genius to work out that God wants us to worship Him creatively. Throughout the Old Testament the commands to worship come fast. Many of the worship festivals can only be imagined in widescreen and technicolor. At many key points in Israel's history, the Israelites celebrated, dedicated or mourned in spectacular ways.

A MODEL OF WORSHIP

We do not see many pictures of congregational worship in the New Testament. But if we are looking for a model for worship, where better to look than heaven? The best picture of creative worship I can find is the glimpse we get of the worship of heaven from Revelation chapters 4 and 5.

> After this I looked, and there before me was a door standing open in heaven. And the voice I had first heard speaking to me like a trumpet said, "Come up here, and I will show you what must take place after this." At once I was in the Spirit, and there before me was a throne in heaven with someone sitting on it (Rev. 4:1-2).

Then, in his description of heaven, John begins to build an intense picture: "There before me was a throne in heaven with someone sitting on it. And the one who sat there had the appearance of jasper and carnelian" (vv. 2-3). That means this picture is color-ful. "A rainbow, resembling an emerald, encircled the throne" (v. 3). So there's the colorful character on the throne, and there's a rainbow—containing the spectrum of all known colors—encircling the throne.

"Surrounding the throne were twenty-four other thrones, and seated on them were twenty-four elders. They were dressed in white and had crowns of gold on their heads" (v. 4). Now these chiefs dressed in white, are not, I take the liberty of assuming, dressed in a shade of dull white of the ancient towel variety. No, these boys are gleaming, reflecting all the color that is already in the room. And as if that weren't enough, they are wearing golden crowns on their heads, adding to the brightness of the scene.

"From the throne came flashes of lightning, rumblings and peals of thunder" (v. 5). So you can imagine it: There's the throne, really colorful, throw-ing flashes of lightning and peals of thunder around the room. The elders get involved too; making sure that the spectacle is panoramic.

"Before the throne, seven lamps were blazing. These are the seven spirits of God. Also before the throne there was what looked like a sea of glass, clear as crystal" (vv. 5-6). So we now add seven blazing lamps and beneath them a sea of glass, which would have reflected and magnified all of this color. Do you think it's about time to put the sunglasses on?

> In the center, around the throne, were four living creatures, and they were covered with eyes, in front and in back. The first living creature was like a lion, the second was like an ox, the third had a face like a man, the fourth was like a flying eagle. Each of the four living creatures had six wings and was covered with eyes all around, even under his wings (Rev. 4:6-8).

And here comes the worship,

> Day and night they never stopped saying, "Holy, holy, holy is the Lord God Almighty, who was, and is, and is to come." Whenever the living creatures give glory, honor and thanks to him who sits on the throne and who lives for ever and ever, the twenty-four elders fall down before him who sits on the throne, and worship him who lives for ever and ever. They lay their crowns before the

throne and say, "You are worthy, our Lord and God, to receive glory and honor and power, for you created all things, and by your will they were created and have their being" (Rev. 4:8-11).

Now just imagine the picture. There are the four living creatures, and whenever they sing their song, the 24 elders leap up from their thrones, fall down before the big throne, toss their crowns down and say, "You are worthy, our Lord and God." Then someone presses the automatic repeat button and the matinee performance spills over to the evening. The creativity of color, movement and voices is enough to make Andrew Lloyd Webber weep.

The point of all this is that it proves that God loves the exercise of the creative. Yet He doesn't love creativity just for the sake of creativity. All of the thunder, rainbows, lightning, elders, living creatures and crowns seem like a prelude to the actual finale, which is, in itself, even more fantastic and inspired. And here it is:

Then I saw in the right hand of him who sat on the throne a scroll with writing on both sides and sealed with seven seals. And I saw a mighty angel proclaiming in a loud voice, "Who is worthy to break the seals and open the scroll?" But no one in heaven or on earth or under the earth could open the scroll or even look inside it. I wept and wept because no one was found who was worthy to open the scroll or look inside. Then one of the elders said to me, "Do not weep! See, the Lion of the tribe of Judah, the Root of David, has triumphed. He is able to open the scroll and its seven seals" (Rev. 5:1-5).

On one level this section carries a strong symbolic meaning, but at the same time, it is good to imagine the picture. John sees a scroll, yet there is not a single person or creature in heaven or earth to open it or even to look inside. John weeps because of this but is comforted by an elder who says, "Do not weep! See, the lion of Judah, the Root of David, has triumphed" (Rev. 5:5). In other words, there is someone who can open the scroll!

Here we go. The trumpets start to blow. The curtain opens and there's a big introduction for the triumphant Lion of the tribe of Judah, the Root of

David. Naturally you would expect the Lion to make an appearance at this point, but instead the curtain opens and what do we see? A Lamb. And it looks as though it has been slain. It stands in the center of the throne, encircled by the four living creatures and all the elders (see Rev. 5:6). What a picture. The Lion of Judah, the ultimate symbol of power and deliverance, is the crucified Christ.

We are told through all this that right at the heart of worship, amidst the most outrageous bursts of creativity, is Jesus. At the heart of it all is His act of atoning sacrifice. We don't worship the creativity, nor do we worship the worship. Instead we look to the blood-soaked body of Christ and remember what it's all about.

As the blood drips from the saving Lamb, all the players worship. Once the scroll has been taken, the 4 living creatures and 24 elders fall down before the Lamb, each holding a harp and a golden bowl full of incense. These, we are told, are the prayers of the saints, the offering that you and I give to the Lord. Together they sing a new song: "You are worthy to take the scroll" (Rev. 5:9).

Then I looked and heard the voice of many

angels, numbering thousands upon thousands, and ten thousand times ten thousand. They encircled the throne and the living creatures and the elders. In a loud voice they sang: "Worthy is the Lamb, who was slain, to receive power and wealth and wisdom and strength and honor and glory and praise!" (Rev. 5:11-12).

What starts with a relatively small cast—a handful of beasts and a few well-dressed elders—soon begins to swell in size. In come the angels, "ten thousand times ten thousand," or so many as to make counting an impossible task. They circle the throne, as well as the living creatures and the elders. Then they begin to sing. Loudly. Can you imagine the volume? Yet there is one thing missing: "Then I heard every creature in heaven and on earth and under the earth and on the sea, and all that is in them, singing: 'To him who sits on the throne and to the Lamb, be praise and honor and glory and power, for ever and ever!'" (v. 13). And that line "every creature" includes us! The finish is almost comical, as the four living creatures say "Amen" and the elders fall over (v.14).

Depending on where you come from. Revelation

isn't one of the most preached about books. It seems to me that often the color and creativity, and the sheer commitment and passion of the cast make the book seem somewhat inaccessible for us in the Church. Can you imagine dressing your church's elders up in a little white and gold ensemble and getting them to fall down on cue? Yet one day you and I will be taking up our places in that cast of thousands. Doesn't it make sense to try and get a little practice in first?

When it comes to leading worship here on Earth, Revelation 4 and 5 offer us an indispensable guide. If we can truly imbibe these pictures, if we can somehow absorb them and allow them to influence our times of worship, then those times will surely offer a greater connection with heaven itself.

EXPRESSIONS OF WORSHIP

Recently I went to see Stomp, an amazing group of percussionists, perform in London. It was a really creative spectacle. There were eight people in this show, and for roughly two hours they did nothing more than hit things. Not just any type of things, mind you; these were handpicked items. They used kitchen sinks, dustbins, newspapers, brooms, match-boxes, car covers and all sorts of other things. The performance started with one person coming on stage to sweep the floor. Then someone else came on and started beating out a different rhythm with another broom. More people joined them and developed the music until there were eight people, each

> It is up to the Church to find ways of allowing people to unite their worship and their creativity. And it is up to us as individuals to find ways of using our own talents to worship God.

with brooms, creating a fantastic noise together.

I suddenly realized the creativity that could be unleashed by the simplest of instruments. That sort of creativity is what we can bring to God as our worship. Stomp's show reminded me that creativity is God-given. It exists within each of us—not just the rich, the educated, the broken or the Greek. And by using the gifts that God has given us, we can be creative as we worship God—He is, after all, a little on the creative side Himself.

It is up to the Church to find ways of allowing people to unite their worship and their creativity. And it is up to us as individuals to find ways of using our own talents to worship God. In many churches today, we are living solely off the creativity of people who died over 400 years ago. But there are so many ways we can release the creative gifts of the Church to find expression in worship today. Why not encourage the painters and sculptors to create works of art that will give us visions of Jesus, and the dancers to help us express worship to God with our bodies? We can also be creative in our use of light, sound and unique instruments. For example, at a recent Soul Survivor gathering, we had 15 drummers playing all at once; and other times we use no instruments at all.

Of course there are dangers in being creative while worshiping God. Worship was never meant to be about performance; nor was it meant to make a good impression on others or to bring glory to those involved (apart from God, that is). Rather, creativity in worship is meant to express devotion to God in a new way.

Whether you are exploring worship through art, silence or even cuisine, the principles are the same: Do it for God, make it accessible and be prepared to hold back on the creative genius, if necessary, to make sure that God is the one in the spotlight. Above all, make sure that your public worship is mirroring what you do in private.

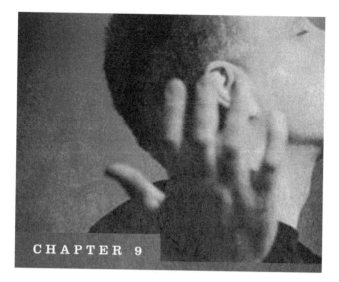

CHAPTER 9

FOR THE AUDIENCE
OF ONE

For those who don't know, the Church in Western Europe, including in the United Kingdom, is dying. Downsizing, dieting or shaping up, whatever way you want to put it, the Church is shrinking. All observers, from social commentators to statisticians, have noted such a decline, and I have to agree with them. Even in my corner of England, a place where many a radical teaching has been made palatable and user-friendly, the numbers have been coming down.

Over a period of 14 years, groups that used to be regularly packed with 50 young people have gotten used to accommodating numbers half that amount.

I'm talking about evangelical and evangelical charismatic churches. Each year there have been fewer young people in our churches here than the last. Something needs to happen, and there's no point pretending that things aren't bad in Europe, because they are.

Lately many preachers have been partial to a bit of socio-Scriptural labeling. We've heard that this is the Joshua generation—a claim born out by the similarities between Joshua, assistant to Moses, and the current generation, who have similar potential. Others have plumped for the suggestion that this is the Gideon generation—drawing on the similarities between the warrior who started out afraid and the group of people that some like to label Generation X. And not long ago I heard that this is the Abraham, Isaac and Jacob generation. I can't remember why, but the presence of three characters had me pretty convinced that the name was correct. Not wanting to be left out, I make my own recommendation: This is the Samuel generation.

Owning Up

Samuel was Hannah's son. Their story is told in the first book of Samuel. The beginning of the book shows her in great distress because she was barren. Her urge to have a child was a desperate desire to avoid the stigma of childlessness. "In bitterness of soul Hannah wept much and prayed to the Lord" (1 Sam. 1:10). She was ashamed of her barrenness, and she went to the temple to pour out her heart to God. She didn't go there to pretend everything was great, nor did she go there to try and forget about her problems. She went to the temple to tell God how she felt. Just like Hannah, we need to be honest with God and with each other; we need to face up to the fact that we are part of a barren Church. The Church does a lot of things, but it is not really doing great things in the realms of baby production.

Hannah was desperate enough for a child that she promised, if God gave her a son, not to own, control or try to keep her son for herself. "Lord," she said, "if you will only look upon your servant's misery and remember me, and not forget your servant but give her a son, then I will give him to the Lord for all the days of his life" (1 Sam. 1:11). I believe that

God is waiting for the Church to say those same things to Him now. We need His Spirit in this generation; we need Him to breathe life over the bones of the Church; we need Him to use us to turn the hearts of this generation back to Him. And when these things happen, we must not try to control, manipulate or keep those people who come to Him for ourselves. We will have to allow them to be His people, not ours.

A DECENT EDUCATION

God heard Hannah's prayers and responded by giving her a son, Samuel. When Samuel was born, Hannah kept her word and dedicated him to the Lord. She put him in the temple, where she would visit him once a year. I believe that God is going to do a new thing in our day, and that through our stepping out and responding to His grace, young people will again come into the Church.

Samuel, we are told, served under Eli the priest (see 1 Sam. 2:11). This strikes me as being particularly relevant for all those churches, like Soul Survivor, that have started as youth churches or youth groups. At times, there has been a tendency for these to start in rebellion, kicking back against the outdated structures of the Church. However, the trouble with churches that start in rebellion is that they end in rebellion. Call it a genetic code. Therefore, in the same way that it was important for Samuel to grow up in the temple, it is also important for the Samuel generation to grow up in the Church. We must love and identify with the Church, and that means the whole Church.

Another significant factor in Samuel's childhood was that he served under Eli the priest. Reading this, you may be jumping ahead of me now, thinking, *Ah, yes, Sammy grew up under the authority of a wise old priest, so we ought to find wise old priests of our own.* You might be wrong—Eli wasn't exactly Einstein. He was so self-indulgent that he died when he fell back in his chair and broke his neck (see 1 Sam. 4:18). Like Samuel, we don't have a choice about the Church. We may well look at it and feel embarrassed, repulsed even, but being a Christian means being part of God's family, morons and all. Samuel grew up learning obedience and respect, and we must learn the same.

So it wasn't all plain sailing in the temple. Eli's sons, Hophni and Phinehas, were sinners. In fact, verse 12 of chapter 2 describes them as "wicked men" who had "no regard for the Lord." They desecrated the house of God "by having sex with the women who served at the entrance to the Tent of Meeting" (1 Sam. 2:22). But there's more:

> Now it was the practice of the priests with the people that whenever anyone offered a sacrifice and while the meat was being boiled, the servant of the priest would come with a three-pronged fork in his hand. He would plunge it into the pan or kettle or cauldron or pot, and the priest would take for himself whatever the fork brought up. This is how they treated all the Israelites who came to Shiloh. But even before the fat was burned, the servant of the priest would come and say to the man who was sacrificing, "Give the priest some meat to roast; he won't accept boiled meat from you, but only raw." If the man said to him, "Let the fat be burned up first, and then take whatever you want," the servant would then answer, "No, hand it over now; if you don't, I'll take it by force" (1 Sam. 2:13-16).

Permission to be confused is granted. When I first read this, I failed to see what the problem was—why was boiling better than roasting? I would have said that roasting one's lamb instead of boiling it would be a sign of considerable style and taste. But look at what was really going on.

The people of Israel brought their sacrifices to the Lord as part of their worship, just as we do today when we bring a sacrifice of praise. The priests received a portion of the offerings, the "firstfruits" whether of animals, grain, fruit, wine, oil or wool. This is how the Lord took care of the priests and their families (see Deut. 18:1-5).

Fellowship offerings were shared between the priests and the worshipers. Sometimes the people had plenty and sometimes they had little. But the principle of bringing sacrifices was the same for them and for us.

A custom developed in which the priests got a lucky dip in the pot while the meat was still being boiled. This had the added advantage of entertaining the crowds as they were lining up and waiting for their meat to be prepared.

Perhaps Eli's sons had short arms, but at some point it seems they decided that the one shot deal in the boiling water wasn't good enough for them. Instead, they decided that they would allow themselves to grab whatever they wanted while it was still raw and roast it to their individual tastes.

The big problem with this behavior is that they

How many times have you said something like, "The worship didn't do anything for me today"? Hello! Whoever said it was for us in the first place?

were manipulating the worship of God into something that would be of benefit to them. And that is the biggest sin in the world: to defile the worship of God. It's what Satan got slung out of heaven for, and it is the root of all our problems.

In the Church, we too are guilty of stealing God's worship. This might get you thinking of examples, and many of us would point the finger first at those who carry on with old hymns in the choir and wear funny robes. *Oh, my goodness, when will they learn and become like us?* we think. Being like us, though, can also mean being wrong. How many times have you said something like "The worship didn't do anything for me today"? Hello! Whoever said it was for us in the first place? Realizing that worship is all for God is a major step along the road to understanding Christianity. It's about our ministering to Him, giving something back to the One who gave everything He had for us on the cross.

When we come to worship, we shouldn't check out who's leading and write off the service if the leader happens to be someone whose style we don't like. The same goes for the songs: Complaining that a particular song is out of date and letting it keep us from worshiping show that we have misunderstood the whole point of the thing. The heart of worship is that it's all about Jesus. Eli's sons missed it, and we need to be careful that we don't miss it also. That band up in front may seem about as tuneful and creative as a lump of boiled meat, but boiled meat is what we need to give.

There may be hundreds of reasons why you would want to leave your church. The worship may be slack, the teaching might be overly dry, or perhaps the people are out of touch. But think about Samuel: Not only did he have to serve under Eli, but he also was part of an institution that was corrupt and decayed in the most repulsive of ways. And what did Samuel do? He stayed there. He had died to himself and was living for God, living to be a faithful servant of his heavenly master. We're not talking about a short dry spell here; it was years before things got better. But all the same, Samuel remained faithful and holy.

THINGS GET MOVING

By the time we get to chapter 3 of the first book of Samuel, we see God getting involved. One night the Lord called Samuel, so Samuel went to find Eli, thinking that Eli had called him. Samuel didn't recognize God's voice, because he "did not yet know the Lord: The word of the Lord had not yet been revealed to him" (1 Sam. 3:7). Don't you find it incredible that he could grow up ministering to the Lord in the temple and yet the word of the Lord had not been spoken to him? In a sense, he didn't know the Lord at all. Isn't it frightening that we have people who grow up in the midst of the Church and don't know how to hear His voice, especially when Jesus said that He is the good shepherd and that His sheep hear His voice? These are days when we need to be desperately asking the Lord to speak.

Samuel finally figured it out when Eli told him to reply to the voice by saying, "Speak, Lord, for your servant is listening." These are revealing words. I know that if I had been Samuel, I would have replied to the voice by saying, "Listen, Lord, for your servant is speaking. And boy, has your servant got a lot to say to you!" But Samuel didn't do that, he said, "Speak, Lord, for your servant is listening" (v. 9).

My longing is that we become a Church that listens to the voice of the Lord. It seems to me that it was when Samuel started to hear God that things really began to take off for him. For one thing, Samuel was used by God to sort out Eli's sons. God told him to go tell Eli that he and his sons had sinned greatly against God and that they would die as a result. Going to your boss and telling him that his sons are due for annihilation is bound to be a trifle nerve-racking. Samuel, however, was faithful, though understandably nervous.

> "What was it he [the Lord] said to you?" Eli asked. "Do not hide it from me. May God deal with you, be it ever so severely, if you hide from me anything he told you." So Samuel told him everything, hiding nothing

from him. Then Eli said, "He is the Lord; let him do what is good in his eyes" (1 Sam. 3:17-18).

I believe that as God does a new thing with this generation, He will give them words to speak to the leadership of the Church. They may be tough words, perhaps even on a par with Samuel's, so it is vital that these youth be rooted in the Church and able to hear God's voice clearly. I believe that the renewal of the Church will come through the young people of the Church.

I heard a story about a youth group that came to our Soul Survivor festival one year. They came from a very traditional church, and most of them wouldn't even have considered themselves Christians when they arrived. During the festival, God met with them and did some wonderful things. The youth went back to their church, and on their first Sunday back, the pastor asked them if they wanted to share what happened to them. As they started to say what had happened, many of the people in the congregation began to weep at the change they could see in them. They heard their children saying things that they never thought they'd hear them say. One of the young people asked if the group could pray for the rest of the church. They moved along the pews, praying for the people. This brought renewal to the church; it brought life. I received a letter from their pastor, telling how his church had been transformed. He believed that it couldn't have happened any other way.

The Samuel generation may not declare that people have to die, but they surely will point to things that need radical change. This brings to mind my Things I Would Abolish in the Church List, but it also conjures up a certain degree of fear. Deep down, I am sure that God is less bothered about what I perceive as being the sins of the Church and more concerned with my personal, well-ignored faults. And so we need to be ready to hear God's voice. He may say that it is time for some things to die that I want to stay as they are.

THE POINT OF IT ALL

Samuel's birth was miraculous. His childhood was something special, and his role as receiver of God's word wasn't exactly mundane. He became a prophet to the nation of Israel. Correction: He became *the* prophet to the nation of Israel. Why? What, you may ask, did such a great pedigree lead up to? The culmination of his life's work was this: One day God told him to go into a little town to meet a guy with a lady's name and to anoint his youngest son to be king of Israel. That

> We have to encourage those that go after us. We need to make space for them. We need to pray for them, to anoint them and to bless them. We need to encourage them and to mentor them.

was it. He went to Bethlehem, asked Jesse to show him his family and poured a jug of olive oil over David's head. That was Samuel's life's mission, the high point of everything he did. Forgive my rudeness, but is that it? Was there nothing more significant, nothing more powerful? If it had been me, I would certainly have hesitated when it came to anointing David as king; surely a miraculous birth, chats with God and an upbringing in the temple trumped sheep and a few teenage songs written for the harp?

Perhaps part of the calling of the Samuel generation is to emulate this final characteristic. God save us from trying to be something that we're not called to be, from trying to do something that we're not called to do. We have to encourage those who go after us. We need to make space for them. We need to pray for them, to anoint them and to bless them. We need to encourage them and to mentor them. We need to realize that we are a Samuel and not a David. What a tragedy it would have been if Samuel had refused to anoint David because of his own ambition. Samuel grew up hearing the voice of the Lord, and the event at Bethlehem was his biggest test. "Are you in it for My purposes or are you in it for your own glory?" says the Lord. It is all about humility, humility and humility.

My former boss and permanent friend, David Pytches, was bishop of Chile, Bolivia and Peru for 13 years. He then came back to England, where he was the pastor of St. Andrew's, Chorleywood, for 19 years. While he was at St. Andrew's, he started a festival called New Wine, which has had a huge impact on many churches in the United Kingdom. Seven and a half thousand people have been going to that festival just about every year since 1989. Soul

Survivor, the festival, the church, the various ministries and everything else under the banner, have come under his authority and were started with his permission. He's even written books that have sold many, unlike mine.

In 1996 David retired as the pastor of St. Andrew's; and since then, on a Sunday when he's not traveling, he sits near the front at our church in Watford. When he's not feeling too tired, he comes and sits at the back in the evening service. When it comes to the ministry time, he's one of the first to go to the front to pray for people. Sometimes I phone him up or I go round and ask him how he thinks things are going. He usually says, "Well, now that you ask, I do wonder about this" or "I'm not sure you should be doing that." But he usually ends up by saying, "But you're the pastor. Do whatever you think." I pray to God that if I ever get to David's age, I will have half the humility that he has. And it's not as though he doesn't care; he gets really excited when things go well, and he gets quite upset when they don't go so well. It amazes me that he just comes to serve. David is someone who has learned to be a Samuel.

In the early days, when we had just done our first

Soul Survivor festival, we met a musician Kevin Prosch, and we were very enamored with him. I went to David to ask permission to put together a week-long tour of worship venues with Kevin and his band. David asked me again and again if I was sure, as it all sounded very expensive and problematic. My charm won through in the end, and he gave it his support.

Well, I miscalculated. Kevin was fantastic, but I booked venues that were too big, with a PA system that was too expensive. By the end of the week, we had lost £15,000 (nearly $29,000). It hurts even now to think about it. I was completely devastated. I went to David and offered my resignation. "What are you talking about?" he said. "I'm the boss; I made the final decision to do it. If anyone takes the blame, it's me, not you. I was fully aware of the facts and I said to do it, so you've got nothing to worry about."

I know from other experiences that if it had gone well and we hadn't lost £15,000, David wouldn't have said, "I'm the boss; I made the final decision. Let my name go on the press release." David would have kept completely quiet.

I want to be that kind of Samuel. I believe that God is calling us all to be like that, to have a generous heart that cares more for His purposes than for our personal glory. I want to be real in my worship of God. I want to give Him the honor and glory that's due His name. I want to hear His voice. I want to play a part in God's master plan. Do you?

POSTSCRIPT

This book carries the title *For the Audience of One* for the simple reason that when it comes to worship, it is God alone who is our audience. But there's a problem with this idea, which I have recently discovered. In saying that we are the performers and that God is our audience, we give the impression that it is up to God to applaud our efforts. Implying that we deserve something back for all the hard work we put into the performance turns the natural order of things upside down. Worst of all, it puts us at the heart of worship. Actually, God is at the heart of worship; and when we worship, we are the ones who make up the audience, offering our songs and our lives in response to the wonders He has performed. Worship is our applause, our ovation to the God who is brilliant, who does fantastic things and who has shown Himself supreme in the face of His Son. He is the Lion who became the Lamb, the King who became a servant, and the Creator who became the Savior.

Also Available in the Best-Selling Worship Series

The Unquenchable Worshipper
Coming Back to the Heart of Worship
Matt Redman
ISBN 08307.29135

The Heart of Worship Files
Featuring Contributions from Some
of Today's Most Experienced
Lead Worshippers
Matt Redman, General Editor
ISBN 08307.32616

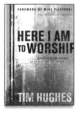

Here I Am to Worship
Never Lose the Wonder
of Worshiping the Savior
Tim Hughes
ISBN 08307.33221

Facedown
When You Face Up to God's Glory, You
Find Yourself Facedown in Worship
Matt Redman
ISBN 08307.32462

Also Available in the
Best-Selling Worship Series

Inside, Out Worship
Insights for Passionate and
Purposeful Worship
Matt Redman and *Friends*
ISBN 08307.37103

For the Audience of One
Worshiping the One and Only
in Everything You Do
Mike Pilavachi
ISBN 08307.37049

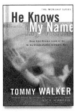

He Knows My Name
How God Knows Each of Us in
an Unspeakably Intimate Way
Tommy Walker
ISBN 08307.36360

Songs from Heaven
Release the Song That God
Has Placed in Your Heart
Tommy Walker
ISBN 08307.37278

Pick Up a Copy at Your Favorite Christian Bookstore!

Visit **www.regalbooks.com** to join **Regal's FREE e-newsletter.**
You'll get useful **excerpts** from our newest releases and **special
access** to online chats with your favorite authors. Sign up today!

Regal
God's Word for Your World™
www.regalbooks.com